ARTHUR F.
BURNS
THE ONGOING REVOLUTION IN AMERICAN BANKING

AMERICAN ENTERPRISE INSTITUTE FOR PUBLIC POLICY RESEARCH
WASHINGTON, D.C.

Distributed by arrangement with

NBN, Inc.

4720 Boston Way   3 Henrietta Street
Lanham, Md. 20706   London, WC2E 8LU England

Library of Congress Cataloging-in-Publication Data

Burns, Arthur F. (Arthur Frank), 1904–1987.
    The ongoing revolution in American banking / Arthur F. Burns.
        p.   cm. — (AEI studies ; 472)
    Originally presented on Mar. 17, 1987, at the University of
Pittsburgh's Bicentennial Colloquium on Changes in the International
Operation of Economic Factor Markets.
    Includes bibliographies.
    ISBN 0-8447-3654-6 (alk. paper).   ISBN 0-8447-3655-4 (pbk. : alk.
paper)
    1. Banks and banking—United States—History—20th century.
I. American Enterprise Institute for Public Policy Research.
II. Title.   III. Series.
In PROCESS (ONLINE)   *HG*   88-1719
                       2481   CIP
                       ·B84
1 3 5 7 9 10 8 6 4 2   *1988 / 63,026*

AEI Studies 472

Printed in the United States of America

Contents

iii

List of Tables and Figures

About the Author

Arthur F. Burns was born in Stanislau, Austria, in 1904. After his family emigrated to Bayonne, New Jersey, he won a scholarship to Columbia University, where he earned three degrees. In 1930, when he joined the National Bureau of Economic Research, Dr. Burns began his collaboration with its founder, Wesley C. Mitchell, whom he succeeded as director of research. At the request of the secretary of the Treasury in 1937, they identified sets of "leading" and "lagging" indicators of turning points in the business cycle, which became the bedrock of economic forecasting. Together they wrote *Measuring Business Cycles* (1946). Dr. Burns was also the John Bates Clark Professor of Economics at Columbia University and president of the American Economic Association.

In 1953 President Eisenhower appointed him chairman of the President's Council of Economic Advisers. Later Dr. Burns advised Presidents Kennedy, Johnson, and Nixon. From 1970 to 1978 he served as chairman of the Board of Governors of the Federal Reserve System. In 1981 President Reagan appointed him U.S. Ambassador to the Federal Republic of Germany. Before and after his ambassadorship, Dr. Burns was Distinguished Scholar in Residence at the American Enterprise Institute. AEI published his book *Reflections of an Economic Policy Maker* in 1978.

Dr. Burns died on June 26, 1987.

President's Foreword

The Ongoing Revolution in American Banking was Arthur F. Burns's final academic paper and remained unfinished in important respects at the time of his death on June 26, 1987.

Dr. Burns prepared the manuscript between July 1986 and February 1987, when he was Distinguished Scholar at the American Enterprise Institute for Public Policy Research, and presented it at the University of Pittsburgh's Bicentennial Colloquium on Changes in the International Operation of Economic Factor Markets on March 17, 1987. The manuscript, as circulated to the colloquium participants and to his colleagues at AEI, bore the legend "Tentative—Subject to Revision." It was, in other words, a first draft, intended for discussion with other experts before revision and publication.

Upon returning from the Pittsburgh colloquium, Dr. Burns requested that an appendix illustrating the paper's central points be prepared under the direction of his associate, Dr. Arthur L. Broida. Dr. Burns unexpectedly took ill toward the end of March 1987 and was never able to return to the manuscript or to see and review the appendix. The manuscript is published here as he left it, with only minor technical and typographical revisions, along with the appendix.

Although this volume is not the finished study Dr. Burns had hoped to publish, it is a singular contribution to the literature on banking regulation and monetary policy in the United States during a period of transforming change; the clarity of thought and exposition characteristic of his earlier writings is fully evident here. Mark Perlman, the University Professor of Economics at the University of Pittsburgh and an adjunct scholar of the American Enterprise Institute, has contributed a special foreword, examining this study's relationship to Dr. Burns's earlier work. It was Professor Perlman, a student and friend of Dr. Burns, who first suggested the study to Dr. Burns and commissioned him to write it for the University of Pittsburgh colloquium.

I wish to thank Professor Perlman, Dr. Joseph Burns, Helen

Burns, Jean Balestrieri, and Dr. Broida for their kind assistance and support in the publication of this volume.

CHRISTOPHER C. DeMUTH
President
American Enterprise Institute
for Public Policy Research

Foreword

The Ongoing Revolution in American Banking is a *tour d'horizon*, offering precision, reflection, and carefully focused magnification. Written by Professor Burns when he was eighty-three but still thoroughly vital in his analysis and a master of historical recall, it presents an immensely readable summary of the problems and convolutions of institutional development.

The Contents of the Essay

The essay is at once a contemplative survey of how things were as well as how things change and a perceptive discussion of what the emerging problems will be. It has five distinct parts.

Section I, "Commercial Banking in the Late 1950s," describes the American system, which suppressed competition between banks and, in return, suppressed banks' rights to engage in nonbanking business. The system depended on its own "gentlemanly" culture, reinforced by the fact and the threat of periodic inspection. That culture emphasized banks' accepting segmentation (geographic and functional), pursuing principally local leadership roles, and serving the needs of their large, long-term clients.

The thinking behind the Full Employment Act of 1946 budded and came into full flower. And increasingly in the 1950s the banking authority, recognizing its sociopolitical responsibility for general economic stabilization, moved to stabilize employment growth in particular.

Section II, "Changes in Commercial Banking through the 1970s," offers brief but careful assessments of a variety of emerging factors:

- the discovery by old bank customers that the previous "gentlemanly" culture no longer served their economic interest
- strong, widespread inflationary pressures
- increasingly widespread entry of nonbanking firms into the traditional banks' preserves
- the internationalization of the banking industry as American

firms looked increasingly abroad and foreign banks expanded their interest in the American financial markets
- the dulling or pulling of the traditional "regulatory teeth"
- expansion of the technology of banking (for example, the speed and accuracy of communication) and of the variety of transaction "instruments"

In offering *inter alia* a discussion of the decline of Regulation Q as the Fed's preferred control instrument, this section illustrates the interconnected, complex quality of the emerging capital market culture and why the drift toward deregulation (law following fact) began and became ever stronger. A part of Burns's genius was his ability to tell a complex story briefly but thoroughly and accurately; this chapter, with all its complexities, is one such illustration.

Section III, "Banking during the 1980s," describes certain changes that Burns called a *triad*—deregulation, allowing ever-growing intra- and inter-industry competition; technical advances, making the system global and operationally quicker; and an increasing rate of innovation in banking instruments. It delineates a plethora of changes and the reasons why they occurred. It covers the processes of "securitization" and "globalization" of the capital market, as industrial firms developed all sorts of ingenious nonbanking capital instruments, banks instituted "off-balance-sheet" services, and savings by American households declined. Burns takes up *ad seriatim* the impact of the second oil shock, the Latin American defaults, the American federal deficit, OPEC, and deregulation. He examines the enthusiasm for mergers, the expanded borrowing needs of state and local governments, the passion for "free" markets and new types of capital instruments (such as the currency swap), and the increasing reliance of American business firms on debt financing. The chapter examines the problems created by defaulting agricultural and oil industry loans and discusses the crisis resulting from the failures of large, critically located banks.

Section IV, "Problems Facing Bank Regulators," builds on the same triad. Burns notes, on the one hand, that regulation was not working but, on the other, that the very elements going into the triad revealed the need for bigger and better safety nets. In the end, he concludes, much greater international cooperation will be needed; he does not see it easily forthcoming.

Section V, "The Vicissitudes of Monetary Policy," is a reprise. After reviewing the traditional control instruments used by the Fed and the reasons why many of them had lost their effectiveness, Burns goes on to reidentify the urgent need for safety nets and the dismal record of international cooperation among central banks and ministries of finance.

Why This Essay Was Commissioned and Its Revision

This essay, commissioned during the summer of 1985 as part of the University of Pittsburgh's bicentennial celebrations, was one of four intended to discuss changes in the operation of several international economic factor markets. The others dealt with the market for technology (for example, fixed capital); the market for information (a recasting of the traditional role of sales practice, that is, marketing as such); and the market for labor (human capital).

Each essay was discussed by two or more commentators, who gave their reactions to the substance of the paper and had the additional responsibility of proposing necessary fact-gathering and institution-analyzing research programs or ways in which the University of Pittsburgh should modify its course curricula to incorporate notice and analysis of these changes. The American Enterprise Institute will publish a volume covering the whole symposium later in 1988.

Professor Burns became ill as he left Pittsburgh and entered the hospital immediately on his return to Washington. It was his intention to revise and polish his paper upon his recovery. To that end, even while ill, he requested that his long-time research associate, Dr. Arthur Broida, develop a statistical appendix for the paper. This Broida did, with the help of Mr. Magnus Ahlquist, Professor Burns's last research assistant. Thus what is published in this volume is the draft delivered by Professor Burns in March 1987 at that Pittsburgh Bicentennial Symposium, plus the post-colloquium appendix he directed Dr. Broida to attach for reasons of documentation.

Had he survived, Professor Burns would surely have fulfilled his announced plan of polishing the wording somewhat (as was his wont). If his reported comments are complete, the manuscript would also have contained more explicit quantitative references. This manuscript, then, was only the beginning of a projected larger AEI-Burnsian effort—one combining his scholarly wisdom and his actual experiences as a major formulator of national policy with his brilliant imagination on this timely subject. What he wrote in this manuscript seems likely to have long-lasting significance (particularly in light of the international capital market crisis of October 1987), because he offered an interpretation of a crisis in the making. But it is also true that what he gives us reflects more than a set of ideas emerging in the

1980s; it embodies his style of thought from the time he became a professional economist in the 1930s until the early months of 1987.

The Relevance of Burns's Career to This Essay

For those who are aware only of the latter part of Burns's career, that part reflecting his chairmanship of the Federal Reserve Board and his ambassadorship to the Federal Republic of Germany, it is useful to recall his immense and unusual preparation during the previous four decades.

Burns entered the economics profession about 1930, when he became affiliated with the National Bureau of Economic Research. Although his first major publication there was his *Production Trends in the United States since 1870* in 1934,[1] the introductions of some other major books of that period suggest that his NBER role was general as well as specific (see the "Acknowledgments" in Simon Kuznets's 1933 *Seasonal Variations in Industry and Trade*).[2]

By the mid-1930s Burns was Wesley Clair Mitchell's principal collaborating associate; their joint work, according to a 1979 article by Geoffrey H. Moore, culminated in their controversial (but nonetheless authoritative) *Measuring Business Cycles* in 1946.[3]

During Burns's NBER career, he was appointed professor at Columbia University. His professorship offered a serendipity. From the late summer of 1947 until the end of 1950, when he left to take up the NATO command in Paris, Dwight David Eisenhower served as president of Columbia. When Eisenhower became president of the United States in 1953, he appointed Burns chairman of his Council of Economic Advisers, but only after the job had been redefined to give the chairman the critical voice among its members.

Although Burns returned to Columbia and accepted the presidency of the NBER in 1957, his place in the political world had been so thoroughly established that he remained continuously visible in it. His political involvement grew not only from his association with the Eisenhower Republican administrations but also from his repeated criticisms of Keynesian theory and policy as comprehensive social solutions—positions he had taken in the classroom and in seminars long before he met Eisenhower. Burns's view of economic stabilization policies clearly transcended his criticisms of Keynes and the Keynesians. His 1959 presidential address before the American Economic Association contained a great deal of description of the roles of institutions in what he judged to be progress in controlling wide economic cyclical fluctuations.[4] To this preferred investigational method I will return later; here let me note only that Burns's policy preferences seem to me clearly to have first emerged in the classroom, not in the Old Executive Office Building.

After Richard Nixon's election in 1968, Burns returned to the White House, where he served as counselor. In his eulogy of Burns in July 1987 President Nixon reported with rhetorical charm how independent and Cassandra-like Burns's function was. That phase of Burns's career ended in 1970, when he became chairman of the Federal Reserve Board. He held that post "for 98 months, of which 26 were months of recession . . . [and] 72 were months of economic expansion. The general level of prices and wages rose throughout the period, but the rate of inflation in both was not very different when he left office from when he entered it."[5] In 1981 he became President Reagan's ambassador to the Federal Republic of Germany. He returned to private life in 1986.

This Essay and Its Place in Burns's Thought

The Substance. Burns was a man of many intellectual parts. I see this essay as his assessment at the end of his career of the breakdown of the remnants of autarky in the West's capital market. He wrote some months before the extreme bull stage in 1987 of the world's various stock markets, but he was aware of the dangers already building since those markets had been surging for the better part of a year before January 1987. One of Burns's intellectual facets was his fascination with "theories" or "laws" of industrial and financial development. For him, however—as for his mentor, Professor Mitchell—theories or laws were intellectually most acceptable when they were presented as abstractions constrained within a particular context. Most of all this essay is an effort to identify the changes and the reasons for them within their contextual constraints.

Burns's "Methodology." In spite of current usage, *methodology* is a word of art; I use it in that sense, which involves why and how one makes his selection of a persuasive device (such as logical models, descriptive accuracy, or acceptability of cultural *mores*). Burns's methodology is a direct lineal descendant of Francis Bacon's scientific method. It bears relatively little resemblance to René Descartes' preference for pure reason and preeminently logical models, the approach now most favored by the economics profession. Rather, like Bacon (and Neville Keynes as well as Alfred Marshall), Burns first observed, then abstracted, then tested the abstraction against further observation, and then repeated these steps again and again.

Burns's passion was for accuracy of observation and only afterward for the proposal of abstractions. Since he was intellectually fastidious about the first stage, there were many (Tjalling Koopmans, for example, in a 1947 essay)[6] who argued that he slighted the ultimate step—theorizing.

To many, particularly those of us who studied at Columbia University with Professor Burns, Koopman's line of criticism did not ring true. We quickly learned that while Burns's work focused on what could be learned from the facts about the evolution of specific industries even more than on the study of aggregate business cycles, he was principally looking for regularities affecting inter-industry price-determining institutions. Once these regularities could be identified, he was ready to develop a *theory* of the business cycle. And, as already stressed, when it came to theory, he asked his students and research associates to be sure to put the abstractions within their proper contextual constraints. Burns's (and Mitchell's) "institutionalism" was not antitheory—it was anti-"quick-and-dirty" theory.

Repeatedly he advised us that in our intellectual journeyings (as in his) connections between trains of abstract thought were, at best, tenuous and, when made, were often painfully difficult. He always counseled patience—more examination of more data could possibly bring along another (and better) thought: better to miss the available intellectual "trolley" than get on one with either an uncertain destination or a convoluted route.

This, his last professional effort, seems to me to show his erudition, his sophistication, and his intellectual caution.

MARK PERLMAN
The University Professor of Economics
University of Pittsburgh

Notes

1. Arthur F. Burns, *Production Trends in the United States since 1870* (New York: National Bureau of Economic Research, 1934).

2. Simon Kuznets, *Seasonal Variations in Industry and Trade* (New York: National Bureau of Economic Research, 1933).

3. Wesley Clair Mitchell and Arthur F. Burns, *Measuring Business Cycles* (New York: National Bureau of Economic Research, 1946).

4. Arthur F. Burns, "Progress towards Economic Stability," *American Economic Review,* vol. 50 (1960), pp. 1–19.

5. Geoffrey H. Moore, "Arthur F. Burns," *International Encyclopedia of the Social Sciences* (1979), vol. 18, pp. 81–86, at pp. 85–86.

6. Tjalling Charles Koopmans, "Measurement without Theory," *Review of Economics and Statistics,* vol. 29 (1947), pp. 161–72.

THE ONGOING REVOLUTION IN AMERICAN BANKING

Introduction

Since the late 1950s commercial banking has undergone revolutionary changes, and the process has recently accelerated. Thirty years ago our banks were mainly engaged in providing their local communities with the traditional banking services of accepting deposits and making loans and investments, and they operated—more or less comfortably—behind walls of government regulation and business practice that separated them from other financial institutions. Today, as a result of deregulation, advances in technology, and innovations in financial practice, commercial banks find themselves engaged in intense competition with other financial institutions in national and global markets—not just for traditional banking business but also for other kinds of financial services, many of them new and exotic.

It is, of course, no great news that an industry is undergoing rapid change; the phenomenon of change has been at the heart of economic events ever since the industrial revolution began some two centuries ago. But rapid change in banking is a matter of special concern. Commercial banks serve, in effect, as trustees of other people's money, and the public interest therefore requires that they be managed prudently. Although they are privately owned organizations, they are the main providers of an essential public service—that of administering our system for making monetary payments. Commercial banks have also been serving as the conduit for monetary policy—that is, as the channel through which central banks seek to stabilize national economies. Turmoil in banking has major implications for the public welfare in each of these connections, and that is why all modern governments regulate banking more closely than most economic activities.

The story of how banking in the United States has changed over

---

This monograph is an initial draft of a discussion paper prepared for a conference at the University of Pittsburgh. Arthur Burns died on June 26, 1987, before he had an opportunity to revise and refine it. At the request of Dr. Burns, supporting evidence was gathered and is included with this monograph in an appendix; but because of his death, Dr. Burns did not see or review the material in the appendix. For additional information on these points, see the President's Foreword.

the past thirty years is sketched in the first three sections of this paper. The first section describes the business of banking as it was conducted in the late 1950s. The second and third sections, respectively, explore the changes that occurred through the end of the 1970s and those that have occurred thus far in the 1980s. The fourth section considers the problems posed by these changes for bank regulators seeking to ensure the safety and soundness of individual banks and the stability of the financial system generally. The final section is concerned with problems in the area of monetary policy posed by the vast economic and financial developments that have transformed banking in our times.

In preparing this essay, I have benefited enormously from the constant and tireless assistance of my scholarly friend Dr. Arthur Broida, who served for many years as a senior member of the staff of the Federal Reserve Board and is now my associate at the American Enterprise Institute. I owe a debt of gratitude also to my secretary, Mrs. Jean Balestrieri, and to my research assistant, Mr. Magnus Ahlquist.

I
Commercial Banking
in the Late 1950s

American commercial banks are privately owned, profit-seeking enterprises. At the same time, they have a very special character. On the one hand, they accept deposits from businesses and households—money which they are required by law or custom to return to the depositor on demand or pay to some third party whenever the depositor so orders. On the other hand, in order to make a profit—which is their reason for being—they must put the bulk of this money to work, either lending it to businesses, households, or others or investing it in securities.

Obviously, no business can pay out money it does not have. Under ordinary circumstances a bank will not be expected to do so; most of the time it can count on inflows of new deposits that roughly match the amounts depositors order it to pay out, and it need keep on hand only a modest sum to cover possible excesses of outflow over inflow.

Under certain circumstances, however, the bank may be faced with a large number of depositors simultaneously clamoring for their funds. Ironically, this is most likely to happen in response to a report or rumor that the bank is short of funds; then, virtually every depositor will try to get his money out before the till is empty.

This, of course, is the phenomenon of a run on the bank. As history demonstrates, the process can become contagious. If the failure of one bank to honor its depositors' claims leads to questions about the ability of other banks to do so, a more general bank panic can develop.

The Scope of Bank Regulation

The banking legislation in effect in the 1950s—both federal and state—had as its main purpose the prevention of bank runs and bank panics. This legislation went back to the National Bank Act of 1863—even earlier at the state level—and included the Federal Reserve Act of

1913, the McFadden Act of 1927, the Banking Acts of 1933 and 1935, and the Bank Holding Company Act of 1956. As a result of these various laws banks were subject to regulation by three federal agencies: the Comptroller of the Currency, the Federal Reserve Board, and the Federal Deposit Insurance Corporation. Other federal laws subjected them for certain purposes to oversight by the Securities and Exchange Commission and the Antitrust Division of the Department of Justice. State laws provided parallel systems of regulation, under state banking commissions, for state-chartered banks. That this complex regulatory system worked reasonably well is a tribute to the ability of the various federal and state agencies to work out cooperative arrangements among themselves.

This legislation, and the regulations issued under it, provided close control of the operations of commercial banks for the general purpose of ensuring their "safety and soundness." Three broad techniques were used by the regulators: the suppression of competition, restraints on the freedom of banks to make business decisions, and periodic examination to ensure that banks stayed within the rules and that they used in a prudent way the freedom of judgment they were allowed.

The legislation suppressed competition not only among banks but also between banks and other financial institutions. The ability of banks to compete with one another geographically was limited by rules on chartering and branching. No new bank could set up business without acquiring a national or state charter, and the authorities were disinclined to grant a charter if existing banks would suffer. State law often prohibited intrastate branching by state-chartered banks, and federal law required national banks to follow whatever rules the individual states established for state banks. Interstate branching was prohibited by federal law.

The ability of banks to compete with one another for demand deposits was limited by a prohibition against payment of interest on such deposits. What competition there was for deposits was confined to presenting small gifts to new depositors or to omitting charges for some banking services. Banks could offer interest on time and savings deposits, which as a matter of law were not payable on demand, but the amount they could pay was limited by ceilings set under a regulation known as Reg. Q. On the other side of the ledger, the interest rate that banks could charge nonbusiness borrowers was limited by state usury laws. There was no lower limit on their loan charges, and so they could seek to attract loan business by cutting interest rates; but they did not avail themselves extensively of that option in the 1950s.

Finally, competition between banks and other financial institutions was limited by restrictions on the kinds of services each could offer. On the one hand, commercial banks were granted a monopoly on the issuance of demand deposits. On the other hand, they were not allowed to deal in corporate securities, to underwrite new corporate issues, or to engage in commercial activities.

Restraints on the freedom of commercial banks to exercise judgment took a variety of forms. There were rules regarding the volume of reserves a bank had to hold against deposits, the size of its loans to a single borrower, the amount of its investment in the securities of a single issuer, the loans it could make to "insiders"—that is, executives, directors, and stockholders of the bank—and so forth.

Periodically, banks would be visited by examiners who sought to determine whether the bank had conformed to the many applicable rules and regulations. But the examiners were also interested in determining whether the bank had made wise use of the discretion it was permitted. The examiners were concerned, for example, with the extent of loan diversification, since undue concentration of loans in a single industry or line of business could be risky. The examiners were also concerned with how well the bank's loans were "performing"; that is, whether borrowers were meeting their repayment commitments or, if not, whether the difficulty was likely to prove temporary. Elaborate systems were employed to sort outstanding loans according to the probability that they would eventually constitute losses to the bank.

While this complex regulatory apparatus increased the odds that the banks would be able to honor depositors' demands for payment, it was still deemed insufficient by concerned citizens. Hence, these arrangements were supplemented in time by a two-element "safety net."

The first element consisted of a source of funds for banks that found themselves short of cash. This source was the Federal Reserve discount window, through which the Federal Reserve banks could make loans to commercial banks that were members of the system and, under certain circumstances, to other banks and even to other kinds of businesses. In the traditional phrase, the Federal Reserve, as the nation's central bank, served as a "lender of last resort."

The second element of the safety net consisted of federal insurance of bank deposits—time and savings as well as demand deposits—up to a stated limit, which has been raised from time to time. This insurance, it might seem, would by itself provide most depositors with enough confidence in the safety of their deposits to make unnecessary the whole elaborate structure of regulation and supervision. But that presumption overlooks the insuring agency's need for limiting the degree of risk assumed by the insured banks; since most depositors are protected from loss regardless of what the bank does, banks could be tempted to take large risks in the hope of large gains. In effect, when the government insures deposits, it must regulate banks to some degree in order to keep the claims against the insurance fund within manageable limits.

Prevailing Banking Practices

In the later 1950s banks were not chafing under the restraints imposed on them by the regulators. While many of the regulations prevented banks from exploiting opportunities for larger profits—and were in that sense onerous—the regulations that limited competition and that provided a safety net were clearly a boon. The law marked out a protected domain in which banks could profitably operate, and the banks tended to stay in that domain.

This is not to say that commercial banks experienced no competition from other types of financial institutions. That was true only with respect to demand deposits, where the banks had a complete monopoly. For time and savings deposits, commercial banks had to compete against thrift institutions—savings and loan associations, savings banks, and credit unions. On the asset side of the ledger, banks competed with savings and loan associations and savings banks for residential mortgages, with personal loan companies and credit unions for loans to households, with sales finance companies for purchase-related loans to households and businesses, and with life insurance companies for longer-term loans to businesses.

Where banks had to compete with other lenders, they had the advantage of low cost for their funds, since they paid no explicit interest on demand deposits and low interest, under Reg. Q ceilings, for time and savings deposits. In any case, in the 1950s the competition facing banks was not intense; each of the other types of financial institution was inclined—by regulation, by provisions of the tax code, or by custom—to specialize in a particular area, leaving banks free to enjoy their own broad area.

In the later 1950s somewhat more than half of the assets of commercial banks consisted of loans: consumer credit, residential mortgages, and—most important—business loans, particularly short-term loans. Their remaining assets consisted mainly of federal government securities but also of some securities of state and local governments. The total volume of assets any bank could acquire depended on the volume of deposits it could attract locally. Banks could, however, meet rising loan demands by selling off some of their holdings of Treasury securities. The composition of bank assets thus varied over the business cycle, with loans rising and investments falling during business expansions and the reverse occurring during recessions.

The international business of commercial banks in this period was relatively minor, since foreign trade and investment were not nearly so important as they became later. The larger commercial banks in major money centers—particularly New York—maintained correspondent relations with major banks abroad and thus were able to exchange foreign currency for dollars, or vice versa, with their own customers or with the customers of their American correspondents. They also were able to assist in the financing of foreign trade. Some large banks maintained branches abroad to facilitate international business of these kinds and to provide financial services to foreign subsidiaries of American companies, and some foreign banks maintained offices in the United States for similar purposes.

All in all, the regulations of banks, together with the lighter regulations of other financial institutions, resulted in a segmented financial industry. This segmentation was reinforced by traditional practices on the part of banks and their customers. Banks were dependent for funds on deposits that came through their front doors—in part, because they did not bid for time deposits of corporations; indeed, they actively discouraged business time deposits.

Just as most banks relied heavily on their local area as a source of deposits and loan demand, so most businesses relied heavily on their local bank as a place to hold their liquid balances and as a source of loans. To businesses it was important to maintain a "banking connection." Through personal contacts over a long period, the executives of the bank became familiar with the affairs of the business and the character of the people who operated it, and for good customers they were prepared to extend credit as needed on agreed terms and with little fuss. In return, the business kept its liquid balances in an account at the bank, including a certain fraction of any bank loans—called "compensating balances"—which it agreed not to draw upon. Moreover, businesses were not inclined to engage in what later came to be called "cash management": that is, when their demand deposits—for seasonal or other reasons—were temporarily high, they did not seek out short-term market investments on which they could earn interest. This was partly because of the relatively low interest rates available in the market, but it also reflected an active concern about possible damage to their relations with their bank.

Banks as a Conduit for Monetary Policy

Although banking regulation was originally intended to protect the "safety and soundness" of banks, certain regulations came to play an unintended but major role in another connection: the execution of Federal Reserve monetary policy, for the purpose of combating both recession and inflation. Of these, the most important was the requirement that member banks hold a given percentage of their deposits in the form of reserves, either in their deposit account with a Federal Reserve Bank or in their own vaults. Such a requirement, which goes back to the early days of American banking in the nineteenth century, might seem to be a reasonable means of raising the odds that banks could meet demands for withdrawal of deposits. But, of course, any reserves that banks are required to maintain are not available for paying out. For that purpose, banks need to hold reserves in excess of those legally required.

Nevertheless, reserve requirements proved useful for purposes of monetary policy. Whenever the Federal Reserve wanted to stimulate the economy, it had only to reduce reserve requirements—that is, to lower the percentage of deposits that member banks were required to keep in reserve. Such an action freed funds for additional bank lending or investing and thus stimulated spending by the public on goods and services. When the Fed wanted to restrain the economy, it could raise reserve requirements. In order to meet the higher requirements, banks would have to reduce their outstanding loans or investments, and that would tend to reduce the public's spending on goods and services.

While the Fed did change reserve requirements from time to time, it usually sought to influence bank lending—and thus overall economic activity—by another technique of changing the dollar volume of reserves available to member banks. It did this through so-called "open-market operations" in government securities. When the object was to stimulate economic activity, the Fed bought securities from dealers, in effect paying for them with checks drawn on itself. Each dealer's account at his bank was then credited with the proceeds, and the account that his bank had at the Fed was simultaneously credited in the same amount. Since bank deposits at the Federal Reserve banks counted as reserves, this series of transactions increased the reserves of the dealers' banks, enabling them to expand their loans and investments. Hence, fewer loan applicants at these banks had their requests turned down or reduced; and as they spent the proceeds of their loans, other banks found their deposits increasing, enabling them in turn to expand their loans and investments.

Conversely, if the Fed's object was to restrain economic activity, it sold securities to dealers, who paid for them with checks drawn on their commercial banks. When the Federal Reserve Bank received these checks, it "collected" on them simply by debiting the deposit account of the dealer's bank at the Federal Reserve Bank. Because that reduced the reserves of the dealer's bank, that bank—besides turning down some loan applicants—had to sell some securities. This resulted in a loss of deposits at other commercial banks and therefore in a reduction of their reserves. As these effects spread through the banking system, many applicants for bank loans across the country found they were getting smaller loans than they had asked for or were being turned down completely.

The requirement that member banks hold a certain percentage of their deposits in the form of reserves thus gave the Fed a lever to expand or contract bank lending and thereby influence spending across the economy—in pursuit of the objective of economic stabilization. By restrictive actions—either raising reserve requirements or, more often, reducing the volume of reserves through open-market operations—it could force banks to contract their loans and investments, and by stimulative actions it could induce them to expand their loans and investments.

There is one more part to the story. What the bank responded to was a change in its inflow of deposits; if these slackened, for example, the bank was obliged to curtail its lending or investing, and it did not matter whether the cause was restrictive action by the Fed or some other, perhaps local, development. We have described the banks as cutting down on some loan requests or turning away some would-be borrowers. But banks could, instead, have used the more impersonal technique of raising the interest rate they charged for loans; higher rates would of themselves have induced some borrowers to scale back their requests and would have discouraged some requests altogether.

Although interest rates on bank loans to their customers did vary somewhat in the 1950s, fluctuations in customer rates were far less important than later in allocating changes in the available volume of credit. Having an eye to maintaining their most profitable long-term relationships, banks generally preferred to make such decisions themselves rather than let the available credit go to those willing to bid the most for it. In periods of tight money banks tended to disappoint customers—often applicants for residential mortgages—of the least long-run importance to them, while they continued to serve as well as possible the credit needs of their large, most creditworthy business borrowers.

In the 1950s, then, funds flowed through relatively narrow and predictable channels because banks looked primarily to deposits as a means of funding their loans and investments, and businesses looked primarily to banks as a place to hold their deposits and get their short-term loans. Since international financial flows were relatively small in this period, the channels were confined almost entirely within the domestic economy. Consequently, by raising and lowering the sluice gates controlling the flow of reserves, the Fed could exercise a direct, quantitative influence on total domestic bank lending and therefore on national spending, with relatively small side effects on interest rates. By their lending decisions, the banks decided how the totals were to be allocated to potential borrowers. Although it may not have seemed so at the time, this was a simple system, operating in a simple financial world. Capital was not immobile, but it moved sluggishly in customary channels.

II
Changes in Commercial Banking through the 1970s

Since the late 1950s commercial banking in the United States has undergone remarkable, far-reaching changes. By the 1970s banks were experiencing much more intensive competition in virtually every part of their traditional business. The walls of regulation and tradition that had formerly marked banks off from other types of financial institutions had become considerably lower and more porous and at some points were entirely gone.

A number of interrelated factors account for these developments. First, with the passage of time, both banks and their larger, more creditworthy business customers discovered that their traditional practices were not necessarily in their own best interests. Second, the emergence in the later 1960s of high and variable inflation and its concomitant, high and variable interest rates, led to changes in the behavior of banks and thrift institutions, as well as of businesses and consumers in their capacities as depositors and borrowers. Third, many firms outside of banking, both financial and nonfinancial, discovered legal ways of encroaching on the business of banking; at the same time banks found ways of expanding their own domain. Fourth, for reasons partly related to these developments, American banks began to look increasingly to foreign parts as a source of funds, as a market for loans, and as a means of avoiding the heavy hand of domestic regulation, while foreign banks turned increasingly to the United States with much the same objects in view. Fifth, under the pressure of events and the demonstrated skill of banks and their customers in avoiding the restraints of regulation, bank regulators and the Congress gave way on one front after another. Finally, onrushing technology, in the form of more rapid and reliable communications and powerful data-processing capability, transformed the world of finance by opening up a treasure chest of new cost-saving, risk-reducing, and profit-enhancing arrangements undreamt of even a decade earlier.

Some of these developments—we will presently comment on

11

each of them—affected virtually all banks in the country, from the smallest community bank to the great money center institutions operating in worldwide markets. Other changes, especially those with an international dimension, were concentrated in the large institutions. But some trends that originated at large banks worked their way down the size structure and may ultimately become general.

Learning by Banks and Businesses

A quarter of a century ago, in the early 1960s, the larger, more creditworthy corporations were beginning to learn that they often could meet their short-term credit needs more cheaply by selling commercial paper to other companies, to pension funds, and to other organizations with temporarily idle cash rather than by borrowing from banks. To be sure, the assistance of banks was still needed; in order to get a high credit rating, commercial paper ordinarily had to be backed by a bank line of credit—but this assistance was forthcoming. Also, particularly after interest rates began their extended rise, many businesses discovered the merits of "cash management." Instead of letting their deposit balances at banks rise and fall with variations in their receipts and payments, they undertook to keep cash at the minimum required for efficient operations and to invest temporary surpluses in interest-earning money market instruments.

For their part, banks made the monumental discovery that their outstanding loans and investments need not be constrained to whatever volume of deposits happened to come their way. Rather, they could attract the funds they wished by issuing negotiable certificates of deposit (CDs) at competitive interest rates, provided the rates offered did not exceed the prevailing Reg. Q ceilings. Banks also learned to stretch their available resources by borrowing "federal funds" from one another; these consisted of deposits that banks held at Federal Reserve banks as well as deposits of other financial entities that were accorded this privilege.

These and other fund-raising devices, which came to be known as "liability management" by banks, had far-reaching consequences. The practice of liability management brought to an end an era during which bank lending rates were relatively inflexible, when interest rates played a relatively small role in the allocation of credit among would-be borrowers, and when Federal Reserve monetary policy worked mainly through the allocation of credit by commercial banks on the basis of the volume of reserves supplied by the Fed. In the new era banks were free to "buy" lendable funds in the market; they lost no time in doing so and in aggressively searching out profitable ways to employ their funds at home and abroad. A corollary of the new freedom of banks to expand their assets was the loss of the old freedom to hold loan rates relatively steady; for when banks paid higher interest rates for the liabilities they purchased, they in turn had to charge higher rates on the loans they extended. In this environment of more flexible interest rates, the channel through which monetary policy affected the nation's overall spending shifted from credit allocation to interest rates—that is, from decisions by banks whether to grant borrowers' requests for loans to decisions by borrowers whether to accept loans that banks were willing to grant at the interest rate asked.

Consequences of Inflation and Rising Interest Rates

In the early 1960s, when banks were beginning to tap the negotiable CD market in volume, the Federal Reserve accommodatingly raised the Reg. Q ceiling rate on CDs whenever it began to bind. But by 1966 circumstances had changed; inflation was accelerating, monetary policy was shifting toward restraint, and short-term interest rates were moving up briskly. Along with other regulators, the Fed became concerned that continuing rapid sales of CDs by banks would lead to large deposit outflows from thrift institutions and thereby damage the housing industry, which depended heavily on the thrifts for its financing. Accordingly, the Fed departed from earlier practice and kept the Reg. Q ceiling on negotiable CDs unchanged. (At the same time, to prevent thrifts from engaging in a bidding war, Reg. Q was applied to their deposits.) The action—or better, inaction—by the Fed crimped the ability of banks to finance a growing volume of loans, since the rates they could offer on CDs had become less competitive with rates on other market instruments available to investors. In these circumstances banks found it necessary to ration loans, and many well-established firms were forced to find new sources of funds. A large number of these firms turned to the commercial paper market, and many continued to use that market even after bank loans were again readily available.

Meanwhile, a cat-and-mouse game ensued between banks and the Fed: banks sought to secure funds free of regulatory controls, and the Fed tried to block or at least blunt their efforts. Many banks turned to the Eurodollar market, establishing overseas branches which collected deposits free of regulatory restraints and lent them to their head offices at home for relending to businesses and other customers. Banks used this device extensively during 1969, the next period of severe monetary restraint. The Fed responded in two ways: by imposing marginal reserve requirements on head office borrowings from overseas branches and by exercising "moral suasion"—that is, urging banks not to use their offshore branches as a means of avoiding domestic monetary control.

Banks gained access to another source of funds by restructuring themselves into one-bank holding companies. Prior to the 1970s the Fed's statutory authority over holding companies extended only to those that owned two or more banks. Thus, a one-bank holding company could raise funds in the commercial paper or other markets free of regulatory restraints and then use these funds to help finance loans by its subsidiary bank. In 1970 the Fed finally succeeded in a long effort to get legislation extending its authority to one-bank holding companies, whereupon it applied reserve requirements to funds that banks obtained from their parent holding companies.

A third device employed by banks was to sell securities to large corporate depositors under an agreement to repurchase the securities later—thus wiping all or part of the customer's deposit and its associated reserve requirement off their books for a time. Since these "repurchase agreements" were not subject to Reg. Q ceilings, they enabled banks in effect to pay interest on demand deposits and accordingly were welcomed by substantial depositors. By continually rolling over the repurchase agreements, banks were able to maintain a larger loan volume than otherwise. Initially banks used a variety of assets in these arrangements, but in 1969 the Fed ruled that only Treasury and federal agency securities could be used; otherwise it did not attempt to stop the practice.

Shortly thereafter—at the time of the Penn Central crisis in 1970—the Fed relaxed its pressure on banks by suspending Reg. Q ceilings on short-term negotiable CDs, and three years later it suspended the ceilings for negotiable CDs of any maturity. Although this particular struggle between the Fed and the banks it regulated thus came to an end, several of the practices introduced in its course remained permanent features of the banking scene—among them, the use by domestic banks of the one-bank holding company form of organization, their extensive reliance on repurchase agreements to augment lending resources, their maintenance of numerous foreign branches, and the application by the Fed of reserve requirements to head office borrowings from branches.

The experience of inflation and rising market interest rates led consumers, as well as businesses, to become increasingly concerned with the yields they could earn on their deposits. But most consumers had few alternatives to time and savings deposits at banks and thrift institutions. Negotiable CDs, which the Fed freed from interest rate constraints in the early 1970s, were issued only in denominations of $100,000 and up and thus were not available to most household depositors. As long as Reg. Q ceilings were maintained on ordinary time and savings deposits, consumers had little opportunity to benefit from the rising market interest rates that accompanied accelerating inflation—until money market mutual funds, which emerged in 1972, became widely accepted as a practical equivalent of bank deposits. These funds—as well as many stock and bond mutual funds—offered check-writing facilities, although there was usually a minimum, typically $500, to the size of checks. Thus, after 1972 small depositors could share in the privilege of earning a market rate of return on their liquid balances, although they had to give up the protection of deposit insurance—since mutual funds are not insured. Incidentally, since money market mutual funds invested heavily in commercial paper, their growth provided a substantial lift to the market for such paper.

Market interest rates fluctuated above and below Reg. Q ceiling rates during most of the 1970s; but in 1978 market rates rose sharply, and the regulators of both banks and thrift institutions moved quickly to prevent heavy deposit runoffs. Both types of institutions were permitted to issue six-month "money market certificates," yielding market rates of interest, in denominations of $10,000 or more, and banks were authorized to offer customers "automatic transfer services," under which funds in savings accounts were shifted to demand deposits as necessary to cover checks. At about the same time, banks and thrifts in New York state were permitted to offer "NOW" accounts, under which checks—called negotiable orders of withdrawal—could be drawn against interest-earning savings accounts; NOW accounts had already been available in the six New England states for a few years. A little later, at the beginning of 1980, banks were authorized to issue thirty-month "small savers certificates" of any size paying market interest rates.

Throughout this period of spasmodic movement by bank regulators toward deregulation, there were continuing calls for more comprehensive action by Congress. The response finally came in 1980 in the form of the Depository Institutions Deregulation and Monetary Control Act. Commercial banks had already lost their complete monopoly of transactions accounts, and this act drove another large hole through the banks' monopoly—by authorizing thrift institutions as well as commercial banks to issue NOW accounts. In addition, the act permitted banks to compete among themselves and with thrifts for time and savings accounts by providing for a six-year phase-out of Reg. Q interest rate ceilings. It also reduced the regulation-based differences between banks and thrift institutions by broadening the

15

asset powers of the thrifts, applying identical and simplified reserve requirements to both types of institutions (phased in over an eight-year period ending in 1987), and giving thrift institutions access to Federal Reserve services—including the discount window. Moreover, the act repealed state usury ceilings on mortgage interest rates and relaxed these ceilings on other rates. Two years later, the Garn–St Germain Depository Institutions Act further broadened the asset powers of thrift institutions. That act also authorized banks and thrifts to establish "money market deposit accounts," which could offer yields competitive with those on money market mutual funds and had the additional attraction of being insured. Not surprisingly, they proved to be enormously popular.

The experience of inflation and of high and volatile interest rates had still other effects on financial markets and practices. The wide fluctuation of interest rates in 1973 and 1974 was followed by the development in 1975 of a market in financial futures, which enabled participants to hedge against interest rate fluctuations. More important, the generally high average level of interest rates provided a continuing incentive to businesses and individuals to engage in cash management. More and more businesses sought to invest temporarily idle funds in interest-earning money market instruments—such as commercial paper, Treasury bills, CDs, and repurchase agreements, while more and more individuals became actively concerned about their earnings on transactions and savings balances. These tendencies increased with every surge in rates, but they did not dissipate when rates fell back; once learned, the practice of cash management tended to endure.

Similarly, borrowers became more sensitive to the rates they paid for credit. One consequence was a more or less steady increase during the 1970s in the number of business borrowers who shifted from banks to the commercial paper market, where interest rates for prime borrowers were generally below rates charged by banks. Banks continued to facilitate this process by providing backup lines of credit to commercial paper issuers. Indeed, beginning in the early 1970s they went further; they helped many smaller, less well-known firms gain access to the commercial paper market by providing them with letters of credit that formally guaranteed repayment of the paper they sold. This was an early extension of the fee-generating "off-balance-sheet" activity by banks that was later to become so important.

The accelerating pace of inflation and the spreading practice of cash management had another implication for banks, relating to the way they priced their business loans. In the 1950s banks made only limited use of floating-rate loans and then almost exclusively for longer-term loans. In the 1960s, when the era of liability management began, banks expanded the use of floating rates for business loans of all maturities. Under a floating rate it is, of course, the borrower who bears the risk of a rise in interest rates during the term of the loan. Floating rates were therefore particularly attractive to banks and other lenders as interest rates moved higher and became more volatile during the 1970s.

For many years it was the general practice of banks to relate the interest charge on a floating-rate loan to their prime rate, which was the interest rate charged to their most creditworthy business customers. However, since the prime rate was changed rather infrequently, there were long intervals in which it tended to be out of line with market rates. In a world in which banks were paying market interest rates on a rapidly growing proportion of their deposits, a relatively low prime rate put pressure on their profit margins. And in a world in which the securities market was a beckoning alternative, a relatively high prime rate induced many borrowers to shift from banks to the securities market. One response to this problem was for banks to keep the prime rate more closely aligned with market rates; hence banks began to change the prime rate more frequently in the 1970s. Another response was to set the loan rate in terms of a markup over a specific market rate instead of the bank's prime rate; in recent years banks have tended to use this technique for large loans to their most creditworthy borrowers. The prime rate remains important, however, for smaller loans and generally for loans by smaller banks.

Growing Competition with Other Financial Institutions

Commercial banks have become subject to increasing competition from investment banks and other financial institutions as a result of the growth of "securitization"—a process that consists of the substitution of marketable securities for the traditional bank loan, either when the borrowing is first arranged or at a later point. This process originated with the emergence of the commercial paper market, gained strength during the 1970s, and has been growing rapidly since then. In most of its forms it involves the active role of an investment bank—although, as in the case of commercial paper, commercial banks may also play a role in the process.

One new form of securitization was foreshadowed in 1972 when some finance companies began to issue medium-term notes—securities with maturities longer than those on commercial paper but shorter than those on bonds. In the late 1970s investment banks became active in the market for so-called "junk" bonds. In this market

17

firms with relatively low credit ratings, which ordinarily would have borrowed from banks or arranged private placements with insurance companies, began to make public issues of low-rated or unrated bonds. Both of these practices expanded sharply in the 1980s.

So too did a rather different form of securitization, involving the sale of interests in a package of loans originated by a bank, thrift institution, or other organization. This practice began in 1970, when the Government National Mortgage Association developed "Ginnie Mae pass-throughs"—that is, the sale of ownership interests in a bundle of its residential mortgages. The practice grew rather rapidly during the 1970s, as other government and private entities undertook similar programs with home mortgages. In the 1980s it was extended to mortgages on commercial real estate and to other forms of credit, including auto loans and credit card receivables.

The 1970 amendments to the Bank Holding Company Act also served to intensify competition between commercial banks and other kinds of financial and nonfinancial firms. As noted earlier, these amendments expanded the Fed's authority over holding companies to cover the one-bank as well as the multibank variety. Besides permitting the Fed to close a large hole in its net of regulatory restraints, they had two important effects on the competitive environment of banking.

First, the legislation defined the activities in which affiliates of bank holding companies could engage as those "so closely related to banking . . . as to be a proper incident thereto." While this language greatly restricted the range of permissible activities for one-bank holding companies—which previously had been unregulated—it was broader than the range that formerly applied to multibank holding companies. Shortly after the amendments were passed, the Fed issued a short list of authorized activities, and from time to time since then it has added to the list. Bank holding companies are now authorized to compete with nonbanks in about two dozen activities, including mortgage banking, discount brokerage services, financial counseling, and data processing services.

Second, the 1970 legislation formally defined a bank as an institution that both accepts demand deposits and makes commercial loans. This definition implicitly permitted firms in other lines of business to acquire banks and, by spinning off either their deposit-taking or their commercial loan operations, to carry on the remaining activities free of the regulatory restraints that apply to the activities of banks. Beginning in the 1980s, many kinds of businesses, both financial and nonfinancial, have breached the wall that formerly protected banks

18

from outside competition by creating these so-called "nonbank banks."

Growing International Competition

By the late 1950s postwar reconstruction in Europe and Japan was completed, the external convertibility of currencies was widely restored, and earlier restrictions on international capital movements were relaxed. These developments, together with progressive reductions in tariff barriers and declines in the cost of transportation, resulted in considerably faster growth of international trade than of world output. Foreign direct investment also grew rapidly—largely as a consequence of the prominence that transnational corporations had acquired in an increasingly interdependent world.

These developments led to a remarkably rapid growth of international banking, in which American banks have extensively participated since the early 1960s. As American businesses became more active in foreign trade, our banks found increasing profit opportunities to serve their needs by providing trade financing and by buying and selling foreign exchange—a routine activity involving little risk before the shift to flexible exchange rates in the early 1970s. Banks also supplied services, often through the branches they established in foreign countries, in connection with the direct investments of our firms abroad and their growing international activities. These branches found additional profit opportunities by becoming increasingly involved in the financial markets of foreign countries and in the Eurodollar market, often in direct competition with domestic banks of the country in which they were located.

The term "Eurodollar market" originally applied to deposits and loans denominated in U.S. dollars at banks—including branches of American banks—located in Europe, mainly London; but this term has now come to mean dealings in dollars in any market outside the United States. It was the first of a series of analogous terms, applying to foreign markets for different kinds of dollar assets (for example, the Eurobond, Euro–commercial paper, and Euro-equity markets) and to markets away from home for other currencies (for example, the Euro-yen market). The Eurodollar market began operating in a small way in the 1950s, but it was given a boost along with the Eurobond market by our government's effort in the early 1960s to deal with an emerging balance-of-payments problem through capital controls. These controls included the so-called "interest equalization tax" on foreign borrowings of dollars in the United States and a "voluntary foreign credit restraint program" for banks that was administered by the Fed. One consequence of these controls (the last of which was removed in 1974) was that many foreign entities that wanted to borrow dollars sought them from banks and other financial institutions outside the United States—including, of course, the foreign branches of our banks—to the benefit of the volume of dollar banking done abroad.

During the 1960s, when large American banks were establishing branches overseas, many banks too small to afford branches complained to the Fed that they were being unfairly excluded from a useful source of funds and, more generally, from a potentially lucrative market. In response the Fed permitted them, and larger banks as well, to open "shell" branches in the Caribbean—perhaps involving nothing more than a post office box—through which they could conduct a foreign banking business free of regulatory restraints.

In the later 1960s the Eurodollar market was given another large boost by the Fed's efforts to limit the ability of our commercial banks to raise funds from foreign sources. As previously noted, when banks turned to the Eurodollar market, the Fed sought to close off that source by imposing marginal reserve requirements on their Eurodollar borrowings and by applying moral suasion. Still, many of our banks came out of that experience owning brick-and-mortar branches in London and other foreign locations, with shell branches in the Caribbean, and possessing greater familiarity with foreign banking regulations and practices—which they put to good use. One practical use was to avoid domestic regulations on such matters as reserve requirements, interest rate ceilings, and deposit insurance by executing transactions with American corporations through the banks' foreign branches rather than through their banking offices in this country.

The foreign branches also facilitated participation by our banks in the burst of international lending that was precipitated by the enormous increases in oil prices in the 1970s. The OPEC nations, finding themselves with more funds than they could spend, deposited huge sums in the Eurodollar market as well as in the head offices of our international banks. Meanwhile, many oil-importing countries, faced with payments in excess of their financial capacity, needed a source of foreign loans. Our and other international banks, including their foreign branches, stepped into the breach by "recycling" the deposits of oil exporters through loans to oil importers.

Apart from the oil importers, the less-developed countries (LDCs), particularly in Latin America, sought massive loans from European and Japanese as well as American banks. In the 1970s, when commodity prices—including oil prices—were high and rising, loans for developmental projects looked secure. Banks in the United States and other industrial countries, often possessed of more funds than they could profitably employ at home, were attracted not only by current profit possibilities in the LDCs but also by the potential for long-term customer relations. In fact, some of our banks actively encouraged borrowing by foreign governments—in part because of an illusory feeling that sovereign borrowers could not fail to meet their financial obligations. Most American bank loans to the LDCs were floating-rate loans of intermediate term, and the repayment record was actually excellent for a time. But a combination of unfortunate developments—worldwide recession, collapsing markets for internationally traded commodities, and sharply higher interest rates—set off in 1982 the international debt crisis that remains with us today.

During the 1970s the expansion of American bank activity in foreign financial markets was paralleled by an expansion of foreign bank activity in our country. Foreign banks established offices here—usually by buying an American bank or opening branches or agencies—for much the same reasons that prompted our banks to go abroad; that is, to provide financial services to business firms from their home country and to compete with domestic banks in our financial markets. The United States was particularly attractive to branches and agencies of foreign banks because of the regulatory situation that prevailed before enactment of the International Banking Act of 1978.

Federal Bank regulators had traditionally made a sharp distinction between subsidiaries of foreign banks on the one hand and branches and agencies on the other. Subsidiaries, which were chartered in the United States and considered to be distinct banking entities, were subject to the same rules and regulations as applied to any of our domestic banks. Until 1978, however, branches (and agencies, which differ from branches in not being authorized to accept deposits from American residents) were viewed as extensions of the foreign parent bank and were subject only to state regulation. Thus, branches and agencies of foreign banks were free of federal rules on reserve requirements and Reg. Q interest rate ceilings as well as of federal prohibitions against interstate branching and the underwriting of corporate securities. By the same token, branches and agencies were not eligible for federal deposit insurance and did not have access to Federal Reserve services.

All this was basically changed by the International Banking Act, which extended to branches and agencies of foreign banks the responsibilities and privileges that applied to domestic banks. One exception related to the nonbanking activities prohibited by the Bank

Holding Company Act, and another related to the underwriting of corporate securities prohibited by the Glass-Steagall Act. Under a grandfather clause, branches and agencies of foreign banks were permitted to continue any such activities in which they were already engaged.

The rules governing international transactions were changed in another way in 1981 when the Federal Reserve authorized domestic banks to establish "international banking facilities," or IBFs. Before this action domestic banks wishing to do deposit or lending business with foreign residents of the United States had to rely on their foreign branches in order to avoid subjecting these transactions to domestic reserve requirements and interest rate ceilings. Under the rules for an IBF, banks located in the United States—including branches of foreign banks—can now accept deposits from and make loans to foreign residents free of all domestic regulatory requirements as long as the bank maintains a separate set of accounts for these activities. The earlier diversion of this type of banking business from New York City and our other money centers was thus made unnecessary by the authority to establish IBFs. The Caribbean shell branches, however, were still useful for avoiding regulatory restraints on dealings between our banks and American citizens—and many still function today.

Deregulation of Banking Markets

The trend toward deregulation of our banking markets might be said to have begun in 1970, when the Fed removed Reg. Q ceilings from negotiable CDs of short maturity at the time of the Penn Central crisis. A better date is 1973, when ceilings were removed from negotiable CDs of all maturities and—more important—when this country and others shifted from fixed to flexible foreign exchange rates. The trend continued in 1974, when the "voluntary foreign credit restraint program" and other capital controls dating from the mid-1960s were discontinued, and over the rest of the decade as banking regulators made one concession after another to market pressures on deposit interest rate ceilings.

During this period and into the 1980s another kind of regulatory barrier—that limiting competition on a geographic basis—also began to give way before market pressures. Many large banks established "loan production offices" outside their home states. Technically, these offices do not engage in banking; their function is to arrange for the home office to make the loan or accept the deposit, but the practical difference may not be great. Many bank holding companies also acquired or established nonbanking subsidiaries in other states, and many have recently used the nonbank bank device to carry on some kinds of banking business out of state. Increasingly, banks have come to share interstate networks of automatic teller machines (ATMs) through which their customers can carry out a variety of banking transactions across state lines. By advertising and distributing their credit cards throughout the country, some banks have also been able to operate in a national consumer credit market.

Furthermore, an impetus to deregulation has also come from state governments, which sought, among other reasons, to attract capital for economic development and to facilitate takeovers or mergers of troubled banks and thrift institutions. Many states have thus lowered their barriers to entry of banks owned by out-of-state holding companies. These actions speeded up after a Supreme Court decision in 1985 that approved compacts confined to a regional group of states.

Onrush of Technology and Financial Innovation

Along with many other economic activities, banking was converted during recent decades from a labor-intensive to a capital-intensive activity by the advent of the computer. Continuing technological advances in computers and communications have steadily reduced the cost of carrying out transactions, maintaining records, and performing other functions required in the conduct of banking. But advances in technology have done more than this; they have also made possible operations and functions that previously were impossible. More than anything else, financial innovation, riding on the back of technological advance, has transformed the nature of banking and of the financial services industry generally.

Thus, the Clearing House Interbank Payments System (CHIPS), which was activated in 1970 to facilitate the rapid international transfer of funds, has proved to be critically important to the development of the Eurodollar market. Similarly, transactions in U.S. government securities could never have reached their present gigantic proportions without an electronic wire system such as the Federal Reserve banks operate. Monetary payments generally have been enormously speeded by the use of electronic transfers rather than the sending of paper through the mails. Money market mutual funds for ordinary citizens would not have been possible without computers capable of handling an enormous volume of relatively small transactions. Computer and communications technology facilitated cash management by large corporations and the securitization of mortgage loans, besides the massive trading in government securities and various other developments of the 1970s. But technology and financial innovation did not reach their full flowering until the 1980s.

III
Banking during the 1980s

Banking Situation at Beginning of Decade

In the late 1950s commercial banking in the United States was largely a domestic—and often an entirely local—business; competition was limited by regulation; and banking practices were governed by traditional relations with customers and the dictates of bank supervisors. By 1980 banking had changed fundamentally. In the new era banks found themselves competing vigorously at home and abroad for the business of depositors and borrowers who were becoming more sophisticated, whose needs were growing more complex, whose options for meeting their needs were continually expanding, and whose decisions were now likely to turn on fractions of a percentage point in interest rates rather than on number of years of personal acquaintance.

Commercial banks found themselves competing vigorously not only with other domestic banks and thrifts but also with investment banks, finance companies, and other financial institutions. The large money center banks were also locked in competition with banks abroad and with their subsidiaries and branches in this country. Much of the competition still involved traditional banking—the taking of deposits and the making of loans. Much, however, also involved activities formerly prohibited to banks but now permitted to banking organizations that used the holding company form—as the great majority were doing by 1980. And an increasing part of the competition involved services of a kind practically unknown a quarter-century earlier—services that had been found useful to participants in financial markets.

Besides facing more intense competition, American commercial banks, along with the rest of the financial services industry, were caught up by 1980 in processes of securitization and globalization. Banks of all sizes had begun in the 1970s to securitize loans by disposing through Ginnie Mae and similar pass-through programs of many residential mortgages that they had previously originated and often still continued to service. Large banks were going global by aggressively pursuing business in the Eurodollar market and by lending in heavy volume to the LDCs. Money center banks were introducing many smaller banks to the attractions of global banking by selling them participations in their foreign loans. At the same time, many domestic borrowers began to securitize by shifting from banks to domestic securities markets as a source of funds; many large borrowers looked for their financing to banks abroad as well as here; and the largest and most creditworthy firms began to securitize on a global scale by shifting from banks or from domestic securities markets to international securities markets.

For American commercial banks, particularly the larger banks, these developments meant substantial changes in the kind of activities in which they engaged and in the kind of loans they carried on their books. These developments also meant a shift of a part of their income from interest on assets to fees for off-balance-sheet services. This kind of shift can be a matter of choice, as when a bank securitizes its residential mortgage holdings. But when a bank loses a creditworthy borrower to the securities market, the decision is usually the borrower's. Moreover, the bank so involved is not even assured of compensation in the form of fees, since the borrower may look elsewhere for any needed backup line of credit or for other services ancillary to the security issue.

Along with these changes in assets and earnings, there also were substantial changes on the liability side of bank balance sheets. Most important, interest-free demand deposits were relatively much less important to banks than they had been a quarter-century earlier, first, because households had converted a large proportion of their liquid balances into interest-earning form at banks, thrifts, and money market funds and, second, because business firms were striving increasingly to keep their demand deposit balances at the lowest levels consistent with efficient operations. The relative decline in demand deposits meant not only that banks were losing a stable, low-cost source of funds; it also presented the prospect of growing uncertainty about the future cost of funds—whether raised through the domestic CD market, through the Eurodollar market, or in other ways.

The Economic Environment of the Eighties

The major trends affecting commercial banks—increasing competition, securitization, and globalization—accelerated in the 1980s. The driving forces were essentially the same as earlier, but their accelerated pace and particular forms need to be viewed against the background of the great economic and financial tides that have swept the globe in this decade.

As the 1980s opened, inflation rates and interest rates, under the stimulus of the second oil price shock, were soaring everywhere, and the dollar was still dropping on the foreign exchanges. The Federal Reserve and the central banks of other major industrial countries sought to contain the surging inflation with tight monetary policies, and during 1981–1982 the world experienced its worst general recession since World War II. Meanwhile, in a remarkable experiment with fiscal policy, the United States sharply reduced federal tax rates without making commensurate reductions in federal budget expenditures. The American economy recovered briskly until mid-1984 and has continued to expand since then—although at a sharply reduced rate— and it has been characterized of late by industrial and regional differences in performance that are proving troublesome.

The developments of the early 1980s set processes in motion that are still continuing. Tight money and the worldwide recession induced by it broke the galloping inflation—at least for the time being. Massive budget deficits in the United States helped to keep domestic interest rates, which had begun to descend from the extraordinary peaks reached in 1981, at a relatively high level. These high interest rates along with renewed confidence in our economy and our currency attracted funds from all over the world and led to the largest and longest rise in the external value of the dollar since exchange rates had begun to float in the early 1970s. The sharp appreciation of the dollar triggered a surge in imports, a fall in exports, and a resulting huge deficit in our international current account, which in just a few years has succeeded in reversing the external position of the United States from the world's largest creditor to the world's largest debtor.

The world economy taken as a whole has recovered—although rather sluggishly—from the deep recession of a few years ago. Many Latin American and African countries nevertheless remain depressed. Inflation has remained subdued in the United States and other industrial countries, and interest rates around the world have been trending downward. In the past two years the foreign exchange value of the American dollar has largely reversed its earlier long run-up. The deficits in our federal budget and current account still remain enormous, and real interest rates—that is, market rates less the prevailing inflation rate—are still fairly high by historical standards.

The huge federal budget deficits of recent years have been accompanied by a dramatic increase of debt on the part of business firms, state and local governments, and households. In the quarter-century prior to 1980, the aggregate of public and private indebtedness roughly paralleled the growth of the gross national product, so that, except for minor fluctuations, the ratio of the former to the latter was practically constant. The sudden explosion of this ratio since 1980 is perhaps the most arresting, if not also the most worrisome, feature of our credit markets in recent years; for it may spell serious trouble for both borrowers and lenders in the event of an early business recession.

To be sure, more or less comforting explanations can be cited for the rapid growth of debt in individual economic sectors. For example, while business borrowing has of late been considerably larger than needed for financing investment in fixed capital and inventories, much of the total has been used to finance the heavy volume of equity retirements associated with the ongoing wave of mergers, acquisitions, leveraged buyouts, and share repurchases. Again, state and local governments have recently resorted for a variety of reasons to heavy anticipatory borrowing and then relent the funds that they did not immediately need. But despite these and other special explanations, some common factors probably underlie the rapid and widely diffused expansion of debt during the 1980s—among them, the greater accessibility of credit, the greater variety of repayment options, perhaps also expectations of some renewed inflation, and a fundamental change in the attitudes of people toward debt. In any event, it is entirely clear, first, that the massive federal deficits of recent years are not the only cause of our heavy reliance on foreign capital and, second, that the debt explosion of the 1980s—and the decline in the quality of debt that seems to have accompanied it—urgently require thorough empirical investigation.

The Banking Environment of the Eighties

The wide swings in overall production in our country since 1980, combined with the sharp slowing of inflation—indeed, with actual declines in many commodity prices—and high real interest rates, created grave difficulties for many market participants who had borrowed heavily from commercial banks during the 1970s in the expectation that economic growth and inflation would remain rapid. Domestically, these participants were mainly in the farming, energy, and commercial real estate sectors; abroad, they were governments and private firms in LDCs, particularly in Latin America. The disappointed expectations that created problems for borrowers in servicing their loans in turn created problems for their banks. Indeed, they resulted in the highest rates of bank failure since the Great Depression of the 1930s, besides a reduction in the credit ratings of many solvent banks—including some of our nation's largest. And serious though the problems of some commercial banks have been, the problems of thrift institutions have, on the whole, been still worse.

The great majority of our commercial banks, however, have remained financially sound, have managed to strengthen their capital positions, and have responded in many other ways to the opportunities as well as the difficulties brought on by an unstable economic environment. Earlier there had been a heavy flow of international credit to the LDCs. This was partly in the form of a recycling of surplus OPEC funds to oil-importing LDCs in which American banks actively participated. The recycling process ended in 1982 with the disappearance of OPEC's surpluses and of the capacity of many LDCs to service debt on schedule. Earlier also, there had been a heavy flow of development loans to LDCs—both to importers and exporters of oil—from European and Japanese as well as from American international banks. This was succeeded in the 1980s by a new process in which American banks repatriated funds from abroad, while financial institutions and individuals in Europe, Japan, and other countries poured funds into the United States. With interest rates still relatively high and fluctuating widely and foreign exchange rates also increasingly volatile, the forces that impinged on commercial banks during the 1970s intensified during the turbulent 1980s. Great strides toward meeting efficiently the demands of the marketplace were thus necessary and were in fact made by commercial banks in response to continuing deregulation and technological advances, as well as through bold innovation in financing arrangements.

The trend toward financial market deregulation continued apace in the United States during the 1980s, and it spread rapidly to other industrial countries. Some of the measures taken abroad, like those taken here, amounted to bowing to the inevitable; once market participants found ways around existing regulations, it was useless and often counterproductive to leave those regulations in place.

But other factors were also at work. Financial market deregulation was consistent with the philosophical preference of newly elected conservative governments in the United States, the United Kingdom, and Canada—and more recently France—for free markets generally. Moreover, the government of the United States, even more than that of other industrial countries that were running budget deficits, had a financial interest in facilitating purchases of its obligations by foreign lenders. Consequently, legislation was passed in 1984 that repealed the 30 percent withholding tax on foreign earnings of interest on securities issued here; this legislation also authorized federal and

29

other issuers to offer bearer securities to foreign investors, in place of the registered form required for issues to domestic investors. In addition, our government exerted pressure on some countries—most importantly Japan—to remove constraints on purchases of foreign securities by their nationals.

Whatever the reasons for particular deregulatory measures, they resulted in greater mobility of capital both within countries and across borders. The appearance of new competitors in formerly isolated markets has had its usual effect of lowering costs and prices. More generally, the reduction of governmental barriers to the flow of funds appears to have resulted in more efficient financial markets, simultaneously reducing costs to borrowers and raising returns to ultimate lenders.

Powerful advances in technology reinforced the effects of deregulation. They permitted information about beckoning business opportunities to travel with ever greater speed to more and more places. In fact, improvements in telecommunications have by now made possible the virtually instantaneous spread around the world of the terms on which many investments can be made or funds can be raised. Moreover, speedier communication and increasingly sophisticated computers have enormously reduced the cost of arranging the best terms on which financial transactions can be consummated. Modern technology has thus linked what formerly were many separate financial markets into an integrated world market—although obstacles still remain, particularly in the case of equities.

Computers have continued to play a major role in revolutionizing financial markets. Without these technical aids it would have been extremely difficult—perhaps even impossible—to design some of the financial devices that are now extensively used by commercial banks, investment banks, and other financial intermediaries. It would have been even more difficult to decide what fees or other charges should be required. And it would have been virtually impossible for an intermediary to monitor its own exposure to various types of risk as market conditions changed during the day and as contracts in one stream were being terminated while those in another stream were being initiated.

In addition to deregulation and technology, financial innovation has been a powerful force in facilitating financial arrangements and integrating capital markets around the world. In recent years, brilliant technicians at investment and commercial banks have been devising new—and often exotic—financial instruments at a pace that dazzles the imagination. In his recent book, *Interest Rates, the Markets, and the New Financial World*, Henry Kaufman lists thirty-seven different credit instruments that were introduced or became widely used in the single year 1985. The best known of the recent innovations are note issuance facilities, currency and interest rate swaps, currency and interest rate options, and forward rate agreements. It will have to suffice for our present purpose to describe the "currency swap"—one of the simplest of these novel instruments.

Let us suppose that an American firm contemplates a financial investment in Frankfurt, to be funded by dollars borrowed in the United States and then converted to marks at the going exchange rate. The firm concludes that after the expected returns in marks are converted back to dollars the investment will yield an acceptable profit—unless the mark weakens against the dollar in the interim; but if the mark should weaken, the mark yield of the investment would be convertible into fewer dollars, thus reducing the dollar profit and perhaps resulting in a loss. This firm obviously faces "currency risk."

A traditional method of coping with currency risk is to engage in a forward transaction—that is, to enter into a contract now to sell a foreign currency at a specified exchange rate on some designated future date or dates. But forward contracts typically are available for relatively short periods and could not easily be arranged to cover all of an expected income stream extending, say, five or ten years into the future.

Another possibility for the American firm would be to finance the mark investment with a loan in marks, arranged with a German bank. If, however, the American firm is not well known in Germany, it is likely to be charged a considerably higher interest rate than it would have to pay on a dollar borrowing arranged in the United States— thus reducing and perhaps eliminating any hoped-for profit. What the American firm would therefore like to do is to finance the mark investment in dollars, in order to benefit from a lower interest charge, and later repay the loan out of the mark proceeds of the investment, in order to avoid the currency risk involved in converting the proceeds of the investment from marks to dollars. Here is where the "swap" comes in. What is needed is a "counterparty" in approximately opposite circumstances— say, a German firm contemplating an investment in the United States, which can borrow more cheaply in Germany than in this country. Under the swap procedure, each firm will borrow in its own country, at the lower rate available to it there. The two firms will then agree to exchange their repayment obligations—that is, the American firm will provide the German firm the marks the latter needs to make its repayments, in exchange for the dollars the American firm needs for the same purpose. Through such an arrangement worked out by a financial intermediary, both companies will be freed of currency risk, and the intermediary will also earn a fee.

By removing the currency risk on borrowings for international investments, such swaps make feasible many undertakings that would not otherwise take place. The swap process is capable of, and is undergoing, seemingly endless elaboration. Another important variety—the interest rate swap—permits market participants to exchange interest payments from a fixed-rate form to a floating-rate form. A combined variety—the cross-currency interest rate swap—simultaneously involves both types of exchanges, for example, of a fixed-rate mark obligation for a floating-rate dollar obligation.

Of late, commercial and investment banks have been busily engaged in arranging all sorts of swaps—a financial arrangement that by now has assumed a very large role in international banking. They earn fees by bringing the counterparties to the swap together. They often earn additional income by arranging the underlying financing for the parties to the swap. And an investment or commercial bank may at times act as the counterparty itself, perhaps arranging an offsetting swap with another counterparty at a later time. In the words of one prominent investment banker, "Currency and interest rate swaps . . . have enabled market participants to link all of the major capital markets of the world together. No doubt this single innovative technique has been a major force in the trend toward globalization of markets."

Recent experience indicates that once a financial innovation is introduced by a banking firm, it is soon adopted also by one or more of its competitors. In view of the ease with which innovations spread, financial intermediaries need to keep creating new devices in order to maintain their competitive edge. That they recognize this is indicated by the impressive number of institutions that have established "product development" departments. That, together with the demonstrated ingenuity of the designers in coping with the endless variety of circumstances facing business and financial firms, probably means that the pace of innovation in domestic and international financial markets will remain rapid for some time to come.

Varying Adjustments of Individual Banks

The sophisticated financial devices on which we have just dwelt are as yet largely the province of money center banks and their aggressive competitors in investment banking. Regional commercial banks and local banks have different concerns. For those that have been heavily involved in farm, energy, and real estate loans, the overwhelming present fact is the threat these loans pose to their survival. In addition to recent records in the number of bank failures, records are being set in the number of troubled banks that require close watching by the regulatory authorities. And difficult though the situation has become for many of the smaller banks in some parts of the United States, the situation of thrift institutions is even more serious. Some states have therefore set aside traditional rules on mergers and branching in order to permit healthy in-state or out-of-state banks to take over troubled commercial banks or thrift institutions. Regional and local banks that are more lightly involved in domestic problem areas have largely escaped serious difficulties; indeed, some have been taking advantage of regional compacts to merge with out-of-state institutions, thus becoming "superregional" banks that approach in size some of the nation's largest institutions.

By and large, the local community banks still carry on a deposit and loan business of the traditional kind. Few, if any, of them are involved in the new and complex financial services offered by money center banks—although they may occasionally accommodate a customer for such services through a large correspondent bank. But smaller banks also are experiencing the tides of change. Many are introducing small-scale computer technologies to hold down their costs. The composition of their loan portfolios is changing somewhat as a result of securitizing mortgage loans and—more recently—also automobile loans and credit card receivables. Their consumer lending has been increasingly focused on automobile loans and credit cards; their automobile loans, however, have suffered at times from aggressive promotions by captive finance companies of the automobile manufacturers. More generally, since deregulation has led to a large increase in the proportion of their deposits on which they pay market rates, small banks have become more rate conscious. And many formerly isolated banks are beginning to experience competition from banks that are responding to the relaxation of geographic restrictions, as well as from newly empowered thrift institutions and from so-called nonbank banks.

Among the major banks Continental Illinois, which the federal government decided was too large to be allowed to fail, got into difficulties that resulted mainly from its domestic lending. Other money center banks appear to be weathering recent economic and financial storms successfully. They have managed to strengthen substantially their capital positions—a costly adjustment that became essential, particularly in view of their harsh experience with the loans they kept extending to LDCs until the international debt crisis erupted in 1982. Commercial banks are still forced to reschedule payments of principal and frequently even interest on these loans. Not only that, they are also—however reluctantly—now and then lending to the LDCs some additional money in connection with periodic renegotiations of their outstanding loans. At the same time, the money center banks are having to adjust to the drastic shrinkage of their business of lending to large, creditworthy corporations. Syndicated bank credits, which previously dominated the international credit market, have of late been vastly exceeded in volume by bond offerings.

These major difficulties of the large money center banks are not unrelated. Corporations in need of credit are turning increasingly to the securities markets, primarily because it has become cheaper for them to raise funds that way than to borrow from banks. On the one hand, the cost of borrowing from large banks is higher than it would otherwise have been because of the numerous problem loans to LDCs on the banks' books. Since such loans have increased the exposure of banks to loss, they have led to a reduction in bank credit ratings and to insistence by regulatory agencies that banks raise their capital-to-asset ratios by putting up more capital. Both developments have exerted some upward pressure on bank loan rates. On the other hand, there has been downward pressure on the cost of issuing securities in this country and abroad as a result of continuing deregulation, technological advance, and financial innovation. Where banks have attempted to keep their lending rates competitive with the cost of funds in securities markets, they have often found their profit margins squeezed to the vanishing point.

However, the triad of continuing trends—deregulation, technological advance, and financial innovation—has also been encouraging commercial banks to help participants in securities markets to cope with financial risks. For large banks whose ability to make profitable loans to large corporations was fast disappearing, the fee income received for such services has become important. Fee income has indeed had a special attraction to banks in the 1980s because the underlying transactions, being off-balance-sheet, did not of themselves as yet call for enlarging their capital.

In addition to seeking fee income for financial market services, the large money center banks have been responding to the loss of prime business loans in other ways. One is to sell off loans on their books to smaller banks, domestic branches of foreign banks, pension funds, and other investors—in order to free capital for more profitable undertakings, such as making higher-priced loans to less creditworthy customers, many of whom were formerly serviced by life insurance companies and smaller banks. Another response has been to originate loans with a view to reselling them—a kind of securitization. Still another has been to offer former corporate borrowers new kinds of services, such as worldwide management of their cash flows. Some of the large banks have also been pressing the government regulatory agencies and the Congress for permission to expand into types of underwriting activities and other ventures that at present are off limits for American banks in this country but not abroad. Their efforts have not been wholly in vain.

IV
Problems Facing Bank Regulators

Momentum of Change in Credit Markets

As a result of a special combination of circumstances in the 1980s, banking and securities markets have been dramatically transformed. Finance today is like a river in flood, washing over and around familiar institutions and pouring across political boundaries, reshaping the landscape as it continually changes its speed and course. Although activities of banking institutions may in some distant future again be tightly harnessed and regulated, they cannot be expected to return to traditional paths.

Increased competition, globalization, and securitization—the three interrelated trends that have been accelerating in the banking world in recent times—are driven by the same mechanism that underlies most economic change: the profits to be gained by meeting market demands at a lower cost or in better ways. These trends have accelerated because a new need—to cope with increased market volatility in interest rates and exchange rates—coincided with rapid technological advances and a growing awareness in regulatory as well as banking circles that much of the regulatory apparatus had become obsolete.

The march of technology cannot be stopped, and the process of financial innovation is bound to continue. As competition intensifies, financial firms will keep innovating to protect their market share and, to the extent possible, to enhance their reputation and profits. Even now, the more enterprising financial firms are institutionalizing the process of innovation by establishing "new product" departments.

And financial innovations will continue to spread rapidly. Techniques that are found useful in certain situations will be applied in their original or some modified form to other situations and in other national markets. Many traditional devices—and some that only recently were new—will be replaced by newer instruments. Thus, the securitization of banking assets began with mortgages and has more recently spread to credit card receivables. Commercial paper was followed by medium-term notes in the American market and by

Euro–commercial paper in Europe. Note issuance facilities (NIFs), which recently originated abroad, have more recently been losing ground to Euro–commercial paper programs; the market for perpetual floating-rate notes (FRNs) appears to have dried up; and swaps are evolving in ways that only the most astute financial technicians can follow. This process of innovation, experimentation, and proliferation of financial market instruments will continue.

There is also little doubt that many banking firms in this country and elsewhere will continue to work assiduously to avoid, weaken, or eliminate regulatory restraints on their activities. These efforts have in recent years forced even reluctant legislators and regulators to drop or relax various regulations. New legislation that may well lead to further deregulation—particularly with regard to underwriting activities of banks—is now being seriously considered by our Congress. In fact, much of the detailed control of financial markets is now generally perceived by governments of the industrial democracies as a costly anachronism. The initiatives toward deregulation taken by the United States, Canada, and Great Britain are having their influence; the laggards among nations find themselves under pressure to catch up.

The Need for Bank Regulation

Deregulation serves a wholesome public purpose to the extent that it nullifies or relaxes regulations that have outlived their usefulness or that serve mainly to protect monopoly interests. But the process of deregulation does not of itself discriminate between good and bad regulations. The consequences for the public welfare require careful and objective examination by everyone concerned with financial markets; for financial flows are the currents that move modern economic activity, and when financial flows threaten to go out of control, our material well-being may be at risk.

Human progress in producing goods and services involves raising the standard of living and improving the quality of life. It reaches people through reductions of costs, widening of choices, improvements in quality, and reductions in risks. Of course, not everyone benefits from each such change; a new technology may destroy the value of a craftsman's skills, and the disappearance of this or that product from retail shelves will trouble some individuals. Nevertheless, the historical record of material production is generally viewed with satisfaction in our times, and most people assume almost without question that the general trend of improvement will continue.

The same applies—up to a point—to financial services. From the viewpoint of an individual, a decrease in the cost of borrowing, an increase in the return from investing, a reduction in risk or in the cost of hedging risk—each is an unmitigated good. From a broad public viewpoint, increases in financial market efficiency are likewise beneficial; they reduce the cost of carrying out transactions, permit better diversification of both portfolios and sources of credit, and—perhaps less obviously—raise living standards by improving the allocation of existing financial resources. Whether the gain comes from overcoming a barrier imposed by nature or one imposed by government, there will be losers; in particular, some financial firms will experience lower profits or may fail. But as in the case of the displaced craftsman in the nonfinancial world, these failures should not be grounds for stopping progress.

Nevertheless, an increase in the efficiency of financial markets is not necessarily a blessing. The occasional failure of a financial firm is an acceptable price to pay for progress if the firm fails in isolation; the danger, however, is that in a world of close financial interconnections one failing firm may pull down others, and these in turn still others, so that many topple together. This is the international equivalent of a national banking panic. National panics, as noted in section I, have been generally avoided by industrial countries in recent decades through the construction of financial safety nets. What worries many citizens is that these national safety nets may have been weakened by the recent explosion of financial technology and—worse still—that there is no international safety net.

Risks Attaching to Individual Banks

The regulation of banking has been deemed a public necessity in our country for well over a century. Much the same has been true across the generations in other countries. The fundamental reason for special government attention to banks is that they serve, in effect, as trustees of those who deposit money with them. Although banks no longer have a monopoly on the payments system, they are still its mainstay. The integrity and prudence of bankers, the risks that bankers take with other people's money, inevitably affect the "safety and soundness" of banks. What bankers do may therefore benefit or endanger the prosperity of individual communities or entire nations. Indeed, with the internationalization of banking that has taken place in recent years, the financial stability of virtually the entire world is involved.

Bank regulators seek to ensure confidence in banks by protecting the safety and soundness of the institutions under their jurisdiction. Some individuals may of course feel that this is of little concern to them, since their deposits are insured by the government. Regulators, however, can derive no comfort from this fact, since the protection of the reserves underlying deposit insurance systems is also an integral part of their responsibility. Much of the attention that regulators lavish on individual banks is therefore useful and necessary in maintaining confidence in these institutions. It also serves the larger purpose of protecting the financial system as a whole; for the fewer the number of individual failures, the smaller are the chances that a failure will precipitate serious difficulties across the national or international economy.

A problem facing bank regulators today—in this country and, no doubt, in others as well—is that they must work with an apparatus that was designed for a financial system very different from the present one. The existing apparatus was originally intended to deal mainly with a national system, in which domestic banks acted in traditional, well-tested, and well-understood ways as intermediaries between resident depositors and borrowers. From the beginning, provisions were made for some minor international activity, and in the 1960s and 1970s these provisions were repeatedly expanded as international banking transactions grew in volume and complexity. Similarly, regulations wre modified from time to time to take account of other new developments, including various kinds of efforts by banks or their customers to avoid regulatory constraints. For the most part, however, the modified rules continued to rest on the presumption that the business of banks, including their international business, would be mainly of the traditional form of intermediation between lenders and borrowers. As a result, the existing body of banking law and regulation is poorly adapted to the markedly different kind of domestic and international business—much of it off the balance sheet—that banks are now conducting.

A special concern about the larger banks arises from the growing process of securitization in financial markets. The firms that have moved out of banks and into securities markets are preponderantly those with the highest credit ratings, leaving banks with loans of lower average quality on their books. Moreover, there is a danger that some—perhaps many—banks may be tempted to seek out higher-risk loans in an effort to raise the average yield of their portfolios.

Other problems for regulators arise from the current process of financial innovation. Given the novelty of the transactions in which banks are engaging, their extraordinary diversity, and their frequent changes in form, the larger banks must be finding it extremely difficult to develop a record of experience to guide them along safe lines in current operations. The history of some innovations is as yet much too brief for a firm assessment, and since all of the experience has been accumulated during a period of relative prosperity, its relevance to any future period of economic adversity is uncertain. Indeed, since the enormous complexity of some banking transactions makes them the natural province of financial technicians skilled in higher mathematics, one might wonder how fully the chief executive officers of our major banks appreciate the precise extent to which their banks' solvency is on the line in any month or, for that matter, on any day. What is obviously required is a well-organized monitoring and control mechanism that takes account not only of the risks involved in particular transactions but also of the correlations among risks of different transactions.

A closely related problem for banks involves determining appropriate prices for their novel services. The price should be high enough to yield some profit after due allowance for costs and for the possibility that transactions may go sour. But in a world that is innocent of historical experience the best information available for pricing may be of limited use. This problem is made particularly acute by the intensity of prevailing competition, which at times induces banks to shade their margins more finely than is suggested by whatever rules they follow.

Regulators are concerned about other aspects of the innovation phenomenon. For example, where new products involve chains of counterparties, banks may be inadequately informed about the creditworthiness of some and therefore of the risks in the arrangement. Customers of a bank, being at times inadequately informed about the risks they are undertaking, may inadvertently expose the bank to the risk of their own defaulting. In the process of reducing risks for their customers, banks may be burdening themselves with undue risks. And there is special reason for concern that they may be making excessive commitments in connection with standby credit lines, guarantees, and other obligations not reflected on their balance sheets; for if a serious setback occurred in securities markets, banks could have difficulty honoring the many calls that would then descend on them.

Moreover, in the new world of banking, regulators share some of the difficulties of bank managers in fully understanding the risks assumed by banks in their ever-changing and highly complex financial arrangements. Regulators face difficulties in getting an overall appreciation of the condition of a banking organization that is simultaneously operating in many markets and many currencies. Nor are commercial bankers and their regulators alone in being concerned that investment banks and other types of financial institutions— which are conducting on a massive scale international transactions

40

indistinguishable from those of international commercial banks—are not subject to banking-type regulation and, as a practical matter, do not have access to Fed assistance.

In short, there is no reason to think that the need for bank regulation—or, to use a softer word, supervision—is any less today than it was in earlier times. But the momentum of change in credit markets has made the task far more difficult. The phenomenon to be controlled has acquired an international character, involving rapidly changing and novel financial practices. To control this phenomenon we have national governments that are mainly responsive to domestic considerations. In various countries—certainly in the United States— the structure of banking supervision is not very different from what it was a generation ago when banking authorities, being subject to overlapping and tangled legislation, had to struggle to achieve reasonable efficiency in a much simpler financial world.

The difficulties facing bank supervisors are magnified by the fact that distinctions among commercial banks and other financial institutions are becoming increasingly blurred. At present bank supervisors have no authority beyond banking firms, while those supervising securities firms have only the most limited authority beyond securities firms. In the absence of a thorough reform of the supervisory apparatus for the entire financial services industry, it seems clear that bank supervisors and the authorities supervising securities firms will need to work out effective cooperative arrangements for dealing with institutions that are extensively involved in both banking and securities markets. A division of labor between the two along functional lines, while difficult, should not be impossible.

Risk of Systemic Failure

Of all the reasons that bank regulators now have for devoting close attention to banks, by far the most important is the possibility that the failure of a single major bank may precipitate "systemic" failure—a chain reaction in which failing financial institutions bring others down. Historically, the larger banks themselves have acted as a buffer against financial shocks by playing the role of "lender-of-next-to-last-resort" both to necessitous business borrowers and to other banks facing a temporary liquidity problem. More recently, since 1982, they have worked constructively with the International Monetary Fund in staving off an international crisis that could have resulted from the inability of Latin American and other LDCs to meet their debt obligations. But if the securitization process goes much further, as it well may, and banks thus become less important as financial intermedi-

41

aries, they may no longer be able to extend credit on the scale needed. Beyond that, and as a result of the globalization of banking and the weaving of intricate financial connections among widespread institutions, financial shocks might nowadays be transmitted across markets with alarming speed.

The threat of systemic failure is all the more disturbing because there is no international counterpart to the national safety nets. In the event of a serious threat, the national nets presumably would be deployed. The Federal Reserve, for example, would pump liquidity into the American banking system and open the discount window wide; in addition, the Federal Deposit Insurance Corporation would attempt to shore up tottering banks or merge them with strong institutions. Similar measures would be taken in other countries. But national safety nets differ in their strength and readiness, and there may be gaps between them. Political problems might pose obstacles— if, for example, American taxpayers were asked to bail out a U.S. subsidiary of a foreign bank at a time when our relations with that foreign country were strained. More worrisome than such possibilities is the fact that national safety nets in the United States, Japan, and perhaps elsewhere do not embrace investment banks. Some of these institutions have become so large that the failure of one of them could have serious international repercussions.

The Need for International Cooperation

Obviously, no nation alone could be counted on to protect the world's banking system—to say nothing of its overall financial condition— from systemic failure. International cooperation is clearly needed to ensure that regulations are adequate to protect the safety and soundness of individual financial firms and that they are sufficiently uniform across countries to prevent firms from flocking to the lowest standard. But cooperation in this sphere, as in many others, presents great difficulties. Each country has its own laws and regulations; each has its own financial structure, tax system, accounting conventions, examination procedures, and statistical reporting systems; each has its own history and is attached to its own traditions. To find common international ground in this uneven terrain is indeed a formidable task.

Still, some highly constructive starts have been made. The need for cooperation in the supervision of international banking first became sharply clear in 1974, in the wake of tremors resulting from the failure of the Franklin National Bank in the United States and the Herstatt Bank in West Germany. Under the auspices of the Bank for

International Settlements an international group of banking supervisors, known formally as the Basle Supervisors Committee and informally as the Cooke Committee, began to meet regularly. In 1975 the group produced a "Concordat," which established the fundamental principle that national bank supervisors should cooperate among themselves to ensure that the supervision of international banks was adequate. The Concordat also spelled out a division of responsibilities between "home" and "host" countries with respect to questions concerning the liquidity and the solvency of offices of international banks. A later revision added the principle that supervision should be on a consolidated worldwide basis.

Since then the group has continued to do work of great importance and has won approval of the Concordat from numerous countries. A recent conference of bank supervisors held in the Netherlands in October 1986 included representatives from virtually every country "with a significant international banking presence"—almost ninety in all. The main discussions at that meeting centered on bank capital and on information flows among bank supervisors in different countries.

More recently—in January 1987—the regulatory agencies of the United States joined with the Bank of England in publishing a proposal for a common "risk-based" capital framework for banks and bank holding companies. Among the listed objectives of the proposal are to make capital requirements more sensitive to differences in the risk of banking institutions; to assess a capital requirement against various off-balance-sheet exposures; to recognize that low-risk, relatively liquid assets require less capital protection; and to move the capital adequacy policies of other major industrial countries into closer alignment with those being proposed for the United States and Great Britain. Once this proposal is adopted by these two countries, others are likely to join. Among other benefits, it would help to strengthen international banks, and it would tend to restrain the temptation to move banking offices or transactions to locations that promise lesser or more lax supervision. Thus progress is being made, although it is not nearly as fast as the new international environment of credit markets requires.

V

The Vicissitudes
of Monetary Policy

In regulating the nation's banking system, the Federal Reserve Board shares responsibility with numerous other federal and state agencies. In attending to international monetary affairs, the Federal Reserve and the Treasury Department work closely together—as a matter of both law and tradition. But in the sphere of domestic monetary policy, the Fed has exclusive jurisdiction, being subject only to various consultative and reporting requirements of the Congress. The Fed is thus one of the very few independent central banks in the world; even its budgetary outlays are determined on its own authority.

However, in conducting monetary policy, the Fed does not operate in a vacuum. The Employment Act, which was adopted by the Congress in 1946, states unequivocally that "it is the continuing policy and responsibility of the Federal government to . . . utilize all its plans, functions and resources . . . to promote maximum employment, production, and purchasing power." The Federal Reserve is obviously subject to this provision of law. While the precise interpretation of the Employment Act has never been free of controversy, it has been generally agreed that the Federal Reserve's monetary policy is expected to steer a course that promotes the nation's economic growth by helping to avoid both recession and inflation. The Humphrey-Hawkins Act of 1978 was helpful in making this obligation explicit.

Instruments of Monetary Policy

In pursuing the objective of helping to stabilize the economy, the Fed has relied mainly on its ability to control the volume of reserves available to commercial banks through "open-market operations"— that is, through the Fed's purchases and sales of government securities. As noted in section I, the requirement that banks maintain reserves at a certain percentage of their deposits provides the Fed with a lever through which it can induce banks to expand or contract

44

their lending or investing. When the Fed adds to reserves by buying securities, it makes it possible for banks to expand their loans or investments; and when it subtracts from reserves by selling securities, it puts pressure on banks to contract their loans or investments.

In addition to open-market operations, the Fed has a variety of tools at its disposal. It can change the percentage of deposits that banks are required to keep in reserve. It can raise or lower the discount rate—that is, the interest rate at which it is prepared to lend to banks that may be short of reserves. At times, as in the late 1960s, the Fed has employed moral suasion. At other times, as in the early 1960s and again in 1980, it has imposed selective controls on particular forms of credit under legislative authority that has since expired. But the one tool that the Fed has relied on most consistently and most heavily is open-market operations.

Accordingly, we can picture the Fed as engaged over the years in buying and selling government securities for the proximate purpose of influencing bank reserves and for the ultimate purpose of enabling overall spending—and therefore production and employment—to follow a path that may avoid both inflation and recession. A useful, if obvious, analogy is the task confronting a ship's pilot. To achieve success, he must be skilled in navigating in all kinds of weather; he must be constantly alert to the possibility of a squall or the nearby presence of other ships; and he must be well informed about both the proper channel and the ways in which his ship responds to adjustments to the wheel. Similar requirements apply to the Fed in its efforts to help steer the economy along a safe course. But the Fed's task is more difficult.

However skilled and alert the Fed might be, its knowledge about the channel through which it must steer is very limited; in view of the uncertainties of economic forecasting, the Fed is forever traversing uncharted waters. Moreover, it cannot be sure how the economy will respond when it adjusts its policies, since the structure of financial markets and the behavior of market participants are continually changing. The Fed is always learning from experience how things have worked; but it is never sure how they are working now, much less how they will work in the future.

Changing Paths of Monetary Policy

The emergence of new financial practices in the 1960s and 1970s— including liability management by commercial banks, cash management by corporate treasurers, resort to new financial instruments, and shifts by corporate borrowers from banks to securities markets—

led to substantial changes in the way open-market operations influenced the economy. In the simple world of the 1950s, when businesses relied on commercial banks for credit and the banks relied on the Fed for lending resources, the Fed had relatively close control over the volume of credit extended across the economy. Allocation of the available bank credit among potential borrowers was largely a matter of banking judgment; interest rates, to be sure, played a role—but a relatively small role—in the process. Later, however, business firms learned how to bypass banks in getting credit; banks learned how to bypass the Fed in acquiring funds for lending; everyone became more concerned about interest rates; and capital flowed more freely toward the highest returns.

In this new world of increased capital mobility, monetary policy influenced the economy mainly through the channel of interest rates. "Tight money" now meant high interest rates rather than credit stringency, and "easy money" meant low interest rates rather than readily available credit. In periods of tight money the most interest-sensitive sectors of the economy—residential construction, business outlays on plant and equipment, and inventory investment—bore the main burden of retrenchment; and when easy money returned, these sectors generally revived.

High interest rates are, of course, politically unpopular, and the fact that monetary policy had begun to work to a much greater degree through interest rates evoked criticism in congressional quarters and complicated the Fed's struggle against inflation during the 1970s. The Fed's problem was compounded as the rate of inflation intensified, for the level of nominal interest rates had then to be progressively higher in order to achieve any given degree of restraint on spending in the economy. Moreover, once floating-rate loans came into wide use, a rise in interest rates was less likely to discourage borrowers, since they were not necessarily locked into the higher rate for the full term of their loans.

The developments of the 1960s and 1970s also created a problem in connection with short-run targets for monetary policy. In the absence of a stable—and known—relationship between open-market operations and overall domestic economic activity, the Fed defined its short-run objectives for open-market operations in terms of an "intermediate" variable. The variable of choice was a measure which the Fed believed it could control with reasonable precision and which at the same time appeared to be related with a reasonable degree of closeness to its ultimate objective for domestic economic activity. Through the 1960s the Fed had relied mainly on interest rates for this purpose; that is, it sought higher open-market rates when circumstances seemed to call for monetary restraint and lower rates when monetary ease was deemed appropriate. But as inflation and inflationary expectations flared up in the 1970s, interest rates lost value as a guide to the degree of monetary tightness.

Once expectations of inflation become widespread in a country, lenders expect to be paid back in cheaper currency and are therefore apt to demand higher interest rates. Since borrowers have similar expectations, they are willing to comply. An "inflation premium" thus gets built into market interest rates. The size of the premium depends on the magnitude of the inflation expected by lenders and borrowers. These expectations are bound to differ among individuals, and they also vary over time. Thus, when faced with substantial but fluctuating inflationary expectations, central bankers can never be sure how much of a change in market interest rates reflects a change in the inflation premium as opposed to a change in the "real" rate—that is, the market rate less the inflation premium.

With the spread of inflationary expectations in the 1970s, a significant change occurred in the way the economy responded to monetary policy. In the earlier era of little inflation, a move by the Fed toward monetary stimulation—say, a step-up in open-market purchases of government securities—could reasonably be expected to lead to lower interest rates, which in turn would induce increased spending on goods and services and therefore higher output and employment. In the inflationary era, however, stimulative policy measures tended to augment inflationary expectations and inflation premiums and thus often led to increases rather than decreases in market interest rates— particularly on long-term obligations. Moreover, any rise in spending that resulted from the stimulative action was likely to translate into higher prices rather than higher levels of output and employment. In short, in the inflationary environment of the late 1970s, monetary policy had virtually lost its ability to call forth higher levels of output and employment through stimulative actions. It retained, however, the power to counter inflationary pressures through restrictive actions, as the Fed and other central banks demonstrated with great force in the early 1980s.

During the 1970s the Fed, along with other central banks, began to devote more and more attention to the rate of growth of the money supply. The use of the money supply as an intermediate variable was supported by the beliefs—long pressed by monetarists and increasingly accepted by others—that targeting interest rates was a flawed procedure which had contributed to the buildup of inflationary pressures, and that the control of inflation over the medium and longer run required appropriate restraint on the growth rate of money. The Fed's use of money for target purposes was formalized in 1975 by a congressional resolution asking the Fed to report regularly on its objectives for growth in "the monetary and credit aggregates." In 1978 a similar requirement was embodied into law.

In response to these congressional pressures, the Fed began to report its objectives for the growth of several plausible measures of the money supply. From the beginning, attention was focused mainly on "M-1"—the traditional measure of money, consisting of currency in circulation plus demand deposits; however, the broader monetary aggregates—"M-2" and "M-3"—were not ignored. But soon came the proliferation of alternatives to demand deposits for holding liquid balances—deposits at thrift institutions as well as banks in NOW accounts, money market certificates, small savers certificates, and the like, and shares in money market mutual funds. The emergence and rapid growth of these close domestic substitutes for traditional money required changes in the definitions of the various monetary aggregates and raised difficult questions about choosing the best definition for monetary policy purposes. More important, the proliferation of close substitutes for traditional money greatly weakened the quantitative relationship between money, however defined, and spending on domestic goods and services and thus undercut the usefulness of data on the money supply as an intermediate variable. These problems were compounded by vast increases in the volume of dollar-denominated bank accounts held outside the United States and by the growing substitutability between dollars and key foreign currencies.

By the early 1980s, it appeared that monetary policy had lost its moorings in both interest rates and monetary aggregates. The emphasis on tighter control of the monetary aggregates, particularly of M-1, that had been inaugurated in the fall of 1979 was thus dropped three years later; and having to navigate since then without much useful guidance from an intermediate variable, the Fed has of necessity taken an eclectic approach to monetary policy.

Consequences of the Globalization of Trade and Finance

The developments of the 1970s and 1980s in international trade and finance have further complicated the problems of monetary policy. The international complications can be sorted into three broad groups: those that arise from the fact that our trade with other nations has been growing; those that result from the shift in the early 1970s from fixed to flexible exchange rates; and those that relate to the extraordinary increase in the international mobility of capital in recent years.

In a world of extensive international trade, there are bound to be geographic spillover effects of a nation's monetary policy actions. Some of the American spending induced by a stimulative monetary policy will be on foreign goods and services, while some of the spending by a foreign country that is brought on by a stimulative action of its monetary authority will be on American goods and services. No central bank can confine the consequences of its actions to its home territory, and none can escape the influence of foreign developments.

The importance of these effects for any particular nation depends on the magnitude of its foreign trade. Small nations, for which most trade is likely to be foreign trade, have relatively little control over the course of their economies. For the United States, foreign trade—although large in absolute amount—has historically been small in relation to the size of our economy. Beginning in the 1970s, however, both our imports and our exports have been growing in relation to total output. In formulating monetary policy the Fed must therefore take into account both the effects of its policies on other nations and the consequences for the United States of the policies being pursued in foreign lands.

The shift from fixed to floating exchange rates in the early 1970s added a new channel through which monetary policy affects spending on domestic output, and in the process it has produced a significant change in the sectoral impact of monetary policy. Under fixed exchange rates, monetary restraint worked primarily by raising the level of domestic interest rates, and its main effects were on such interest-sensitive activities as residential construction and business fixed investment. To the extent that capital was mobile internationally, high interest rates in the United States would have tended to attract investment funds from other countries. But such flows would have put downward pressure on the exchange rates of foreign currencies against the dollar, and central banks committed to maintaining fixed exchange rates would therefore have had to take offsetting actions—such as raising their own interest rates—to discourage the outflows.

In the present regime of flexible exchange rates, however, foreign central banks are not obliged to take such actions; and funds from their countries may therefore flow freely to the United States or elsewhere in pursuit of higher returns. In fact, foreign funds have been flowing into the United States on a massive scale in recent years, as a consequence in large part of the relatively high interest rates produced by our mix of fiscal and monetary policies. Inflows of that kind have two simultaneous effects. First, by adding to the supply of funds in our financial markets, they exert a moderating influence on interest rates. Second, by increasing the demand for dollars in the foreign exchange markets, they put upward pressure on the dollar exchange rate. The first effect—the moderating influence on interest rates—means that the interest-sensitive sectors of our economy are no longer punished by tight money as severely as they formerly were. But the second effect—the rise in dollar exchange rates against foreign currencies—results in a fall in our exports and a rise in our imports; that is, it results in a shift from spending on domestic output to spending on foreign output. This means that the burden of tight money is nowadays borne in good part by sectors of our economy that previously did not suffer unduly, namely, those that export a substantial part of their output and those that compete with imports.

The addition of this important new channel for the transmission of the effects of monetary policy has modified the relation between the Fed's policy actions and the resulting change in spending on domestic output; in particular, lags have become longer, and the magnitude of the response less certain. This new development has also posed a political problem for the Fed. The newly affected groups include farmers and manufacturers, among others. Compared with the long-suffering home builders, these groups are less likely to identify the Fed and its anti-inflation policy as the immediate source of their problems; rather, they will see the enemy in their foreign competitors and call for import protection or export subsidies. Even if they appreciate the Fed's role, they are still likely to demand that their difficulties be remedied by intervention in the nation's foreign trade, and experience demonstrates that they are likely to find sympathetic ears in Congress and the executive branch. The possibility of such an outcome is bound to make it more difficult for the Fed to pursue anti-inflation efforts. And if the Fed should barge ahead—and perhaps precipitate massive protectionism—it might wind up with a more timid policy anyway. For with farmers and manufacturers "protected" against foreign competition, any given degree of restraint on overall spending could then be attained only by squeezing home builders and others still more, and that would probably involve pressing interest rates to unacceptably high levels.

The heightened international mobility of capital has created its own special problems for monetary policy. It is now simple and inexpensive for investors and borrowers almost anywhere in the world to shift their transactions from one currency to another or from one national market to another. Huge sums can be set in rapid motion by relatively small changes in interest rates or exchange rates or even by news reports or rumors bearing on the outlook for rates or government policies. This rapid mobility of capital can prove troublesome for the United States, in view of our current need for capital inflows to help finance our huge public and private borrowing.

More generally, however, the speed with which international financial markets can react to events can have serious consequences for the Fed's ability to act in accordance with its judgment about the needs of the domestic economy. Consider, for example, the different speeds of response of exchange rates and flows of foreign trade. Since exchange rates can respond rapidly to a monetary action while the effects of that change on trade might extend over several years, it is difficult for the Fed to determine the appropriate scale of its policy measures. Moreover, since exchange rates may easily overshoot their ultimate level, reluctance by the Fed to contribute to exchange rate volatility may incline it to temper its actions from the optimum indicated by its economic analysis.

Altogether, as the world's markets for goods and financial services become increasingly integrated, it is becoming harder for central banks of industrial countries to maintain national financial conditions that differ significantly from conditions in the industrial world at large. We appear to have reached a stage in the world's economic evolution where central bankers and finance ministers of the major countries will be able to achieve the financial conditions they desire in their own countries only by acting in concert with their counterparts in other major countries.

The Need for Coordinating Economic Policies

The loss of national autonomy in the sphere of economic policy has been reflected recently in the repeated appeals by American officials to Germany and Japan to adopt more stimulative policies; in the repeated appeals by officials of Germany, Japan, and other countries to the United States to reduce its federal budget deficit; and in the consultations among finance ministers and central bank governors of the leading industrial democracies about the course of their domestic policies and movements in the exchange rates among their currencies. Such consultations led to the "Plaza" agreement of September 1985 on measures to achieve better relations among exchange rates and to coordinated actions on discount rates in the early months of 1986.

At their latest meeting, held in Paris in early 1987, the ministers and governors agreed to cooperate closely to foster stability of exchange rates around current levels, which, in their judgment, were "within ranges broadly consistent with underlying economic fundamentals." Much to their credit, they also recognized that the major industrial countries "have a special responsibility to follow policies which foster an open, growing world economy in order to support the efforts of developing countries, especially debtor countries, to restore steady growth and viable balance of payments positions."

The need for cooperation among nations with respect to economic problems is not a recent discovery. Even before World War II came to an end, agreement was reached at Bretton Woods on a new international monetary system, in which a key role would be played—as it indeed has been—by a new institution, the International Monetary Fund. Agreement was also reached at Bretton Woods on a sister institution, the International Bank for Reconstruction and Development, commonly called the World Bank, which has played a significant role in financing economic development in the third world. Shortly after the war a conference in Geneva led to the General Agreement on Tariffs and Trade, which has served as a powerful force for trade liberalization in the postwar era. The European Community, established in Rome in 1957, includes nations that have substantially reduced barriers to the movement of goods, services, and labor among themselves and that are cooperating across a wide range of policies. Most members of the community joined together in 1979 to form the European Monetary System, under which their currencies are pegged to one another. And for a good many years, the central bank governors of the "Group of Ten"—comprising the ten leading industrial countries—have discussed problems of common interest and occasionally have taken common action at their monthly meetings, held under the auspices of the Bank for International Settlements at Basel.

Clearly, there has been no lack of international consultation, coordination, and cooperation with respect to various kinds of economic policy, and the results of these efforts have often proved beneficial. And yet there are grounds for disappointment in what has been achieved, especially in recent years, in coordinating national monetary and fiscal policies for the purpose of improving world economic conditions. Too often well-publicized international meetings have accomplished little of lasting value. Too often coordinated action has been agreed to only grudgingly, late, and in insufficient measure.

The reasons for these shortcomings are not far to seek. There are differences among nations in prevailing economic conditions and therefore in the perceived need for change; there are differences in national priorities; and there are honest disagreements about the causes of existing problems and the best means of resolving them. But perhaps the most fundamental difficulty is a political one. Since governments of democratic nations respect the voices of their citizens, the range of actions on which they can agree with other nations is constrained by considerations of domestic acceptability. To understand the depth of this difficulty, one need only consider how hard it is within our own nation to bring the various elements of fiscal policy together into a rational whole in the face of competing pressures from interest groups and wide differences between the Congress and the White House.

In sum, there are enormous problems in developing effective international cooperation in the area of monetary and fiscal policy, just as there are in the area of supervision of financial institutions. Although the sources of the problems are quite different—being mainly political in the former case and mainly technical in the latter— the need for resolving them is pressing and will become more pressing with the passage of time. Since the world's problems in these areas are far beyond the reach of national tools for their resolution, nations must find the will and the means to cooperate in their mutual interest. Fortunately, this need is increasingly understood by leading citizens around the world. We can only hope that their views will prevail and that people generally will come to understand that our international political arrangements are as yet poorly adapted to the sweeping internationalization that has been under way in recent years in technology, industrial activities, trade, banking, and securities markets.

Appendix

TABLE 1
KEY PROVISIONS OF MAJOR U.S. BANKING LAWS

National Bank Act of 1863
- established Office of Comptroller of Currency (OCC) in Treasury Department to administer laws relating to national banks
- provided for chartering, supervision, and examination of national banks by OCC and for submission of periodic condition reports to OCC
- specified minimum capital requirements for national banks
- specified reserve requirements against notes and deposits; in addition to vault cash, "country banks" could hold reserves at reserve city or central reserve city banks, and reserve city banks could hold reserves at central reserve city banks
- prohibited loans to any one borrower exceeding 10 percent of capital stock
- authorized branches of national banks only for previously owned branches of state banks converting to national banks

Federal Reserve Act (1913)
- established Federal Reserve Board (FRB) in Washington and twelve district Federal Reserve Banks (FRBks) to oversee Federal Reserve System (FRS); board consisted of seven members, including secretary of Treasury and comptroller of currency
- required all national banks to become members of FRS and permitted eligible state banks to join
- specified minimum capital requirements for member banks
- specified reserve requirements for member banks; reserves had to be held in FRBk in member bank's district
- authorized national banks to establish branches abroad
- granted trust powers to national banks
- authorized FRBks to discount notes, drafts, and bills of exchange arising out of commercial transactions and acceptances arising out of imports and exports
- authorized FRBks to set discount rates subject to review and determination by FRB
- authorized FRBks to buy and sell U.S. government securities
- authorized FRBks to issue Federal Reserve notes to serve as legal tender

(Table continues)

TABLE 1 (continued)

- required OCC to examine member banks at least twice each year
- authorized FRB to examine each FRBk and each member bank at its discretion and to require such statements and reports as it deemed necessary
- directed FRBks to act as fiscal agents for U.S. Treasury

Edge Act (1919)
- authorized FRB to charter corporations to engage in international banking and permitted domestic banks to invest in such corporations; Edge Act corporations may not engage in banking activities in United States or invest in corporations that do business in United States unless FRB concludes such activities are incidental to corporation's foreign activities

McFadden Act (1927)
- permitted national banks (with approval of OCC) and state member banks (with approval of FRB) to branch in their home cities to the extent that state banks were similarly permitted by state law; as a result, national banks were not permitted to branch across state lines

Banking Act of 1933
- created Federal Open Market Committee (FOMC) to regulate and coordinate transactions in U.S. government securities by FRBks
- prohibited payment of interest on demand deposits
- gave FRB authority to impose interest rate ceilings on time and savings deposits at member banks
- created Federal Deposit Insurance Corporation (FDIC) and provided for deposit insurance up to limit of $2,500 for each deposit (insurance limit was raised to $5,000 in 1934)
- prohibited loans by member banks to executive officers
- authorized national bank examiners to examine affiliates of banks
- sections 16, 20, 21, and 32 (collectively known as Glass-Steagall Act) provided for separation between banking and securities business:
    sec. 16—prohibited national banks and state member banks from purchasing equities and prohibited their underwriting and dealing in securities other than U.S. Treasury securities, agency obligations, and general state and municipal obligations
    sec. 20—prohibited member banks from affiliating with organizations engaged principally in securities activities
    sec. 21—prohibited a person engaged in securities business from receiving deposits (with certain exceptions for state-chartered banks)
    sec. 32—prohibited interlocking directorates between member banks and securities firms unless authorized by FRB

Banking Act of 1935
- restructured FRB to consist of seven members, not including secretary of Treasury and comptroller of currency
- restructured FOMC to consist of members of FRB plus rotating group of five FRBk presidents

TABLE 1 (continued)

- revised FDIC and expanded its regulatory authority over insured banks
- gave FRB authority to adjust reserve requirements within specified ranges
- permitted national banks to make five-year real estate loans
- authorized ceilings on interest rates on time and savings deposits at all federally insured banks

FDIC Act (1950)

- put FDIC under separate law and gave it extensive authority over insured banks and branches in the United States
- provided for assessments against insured institutions and for creation of a permanent insurance fund
- authorized FDIC to borrow from Treasury
- raised limit on insured deposits from $5,000 to $10,000

Bank Holding Company Act of 1956

- gave to FRB the primary responsibility for supervising and regulating multibank holding companies, in order to avoid restraint of trade in banking and to maintain a separation between commerce and banking by permitting holding companies to engage only in nonbanking activities that are closely related to banking
- provided that a bank holding company operating in one state may not acquire a bank in a second state unless that state expressly authorizes the acquisition by statute
- grandfathered existing interstate bank holding companies and allowed bank holding companies to place certain nonbank affiliates in other states

Bank Merger Acts of 1960 and 1966

- prohibited mergers between an insured bank and a noninsured institution without approval of FDIC
- prohibited mergers of any two insured banks without approval of (1) the OCC if resulting bank is to be a national bank, (2) the FRB if resulting bank is to be a state member bank, or (3) the FDIC if resulting bank is to be a nonmember insured bank
- specified that mergers were not to be approved if they would create a monopoly or if they would substantially lessen competition unless anticompetitive effects were clearly outweighed by convenience and needs of community
- authorized Justice Department to bring suit under antitrust laws to prevent a proposed merger

1966 Amendment to Bank Holding Company Act

- made the factors FRB is to consider in acting on bank holding company applications conform to those designated in the 1966 Bank Merger Act
- defined a bank as an institution accepting demand deposits

(Table continues)

TABLE 1 (continued)

Interest Rate Adjustment Act (1966)
• extended deposit rate ceilings to all federally insured time and savings deposits, including those at savings and loan associations and mutual savings banks

Financial Institutions Supervisory Act of 1966
• granted extensive cease-and-desist and other enforcement authority to the OCC, FDIC, and FRB in the interest of protecting the safety and soundness of financial institutions
• increased the limit on insured deposits from $10,000 to $15,000

1970 Amendments to Bank Holding Company Act
• extended FRB's authority over bank holding companies to one-bank holding companies
• broadened somewhat the exceptions to the prohibition against bank holding companies engaging in nonbanking activities
• defined a bank as an institution accepting demand deposits and making commercial loans

International Banking Act of 1978
• placed foreign banks on a more equal footing with domestic banks by authorizing foreign banks to open federally chartered branches and agencies in the United States; by extending to U.S. branches of foreign banks provisions of laws affecting U.S. banks with respect to examinations, Regulation Q, reserve requirements, deposit insurance, bank holding company restraints, and others; and by providing access to Federal Reserve facilities for foreign banks that maintain reserves at FRBks
• grandfathered interstate branching and investment banking activities that were in operation before specified dates

Full Employment and Balanced Growth (Humphrey-Hawkins) Act of 1978
• established medium-term goals for reduction of unemployment and inflation
• required FRB to transmit to Congress twice a year analyses of recent economic developments, statements of objectives and plans of FRB with respect to ranges of growth of monetary and credit aggregates for the calendar year, and statement of the relations of such objectives to short-term goals of the president and any approved by the Congress

Federal Financial Institutions Examination Council Act of 1978
• created council consisting of heads of OCC, FRB, FDIC, Federal Home Loan Bank Board, and National Credit Union Administration to prescribe uniform principles for federal examination of financial institutions and to make recommendations to promote uniformity in their supervision

Depository Institutions Deregulation and Monetary Control Act (DIDMCA) of 1980
• provided for six-year phase-out of Reg. Q ceilings on time and savings deposit interest rates

TABLE 1 (concluded)

• authorized NOW accounts for all federally insured depository institutions

• eliminated FRB reserve requirements on personal time and savings deposits

• simplified reserve requirements on transactions accounts and applied these requirements to nonmember banks and thrift institutions as well as to member banks

• required FRBks to provide nonmember banks and thrift institutions such services as borrowing at discount window, check clearing, safekeeping of securities, wire transfers, automatic clearinghouse facilities, and cash transportation services

• required FRBks to provide services at prices reflecting costs plus mark-ups

• authorized savings and loan associations to invest up to 20 percent of assets in consumer loans, commercial paper, and corporate debt securities; to issue credit cards; and to exercise trust powers

• authorized mutual savings banks to make commercial, corporate, and business loans up to 5 percent of assets

• relaxed state usury ceilings

• raised ceiling on deposit insurance from $40,000 to $100,000 (ceiling had been raised from $15,000 to $20,000 in 1969 and to $40,000 in 1974)

Garn–St Germain Depository Institutions Act of 1982

• authorized depository institutions to offer money market deposit accounts, with no interest ceiling and insured up to $100,000

• authorized thrift institutions to invest in state government securities; to make commercial and agricultural loans up to 10 percent of assets; and to accept deposits from businesses with which a loan relationship had been established

• increased lending limits for national banks

• authorized various actions by regulatory agencies to assist troubled institutions, including approval of emergency acquisitions across state lines

International Lending Supervision Act (1983)

• authorized regulatory agencies to establish minimum capital levels for banks and to require special reserves on loans adversely affected by country risk

TABLE 2: ECONOMIC ACTIVITY, INTERNATIONAL TRADE, AND
INTERNATIONAL BANKING, SELECTED YEARS, 1964–1985
(billions of dollars at current prices and current exchange rates)

Indicator	1964	1972	1980	1983	1985	Compound Annual Rate of Growth, 1964–85
Gross domestic product, world excluding Soviet bloc[a]	1,605	3,336	10,172	10,140	12,825 E	10.4
International trade in goods and services, world excluding Soviet bloc[a]	188	463	2,150	1,986	2,190 E	12.4
International banking BIS series for net international bank credit, BIS reporting area[b]	12 E	122 E	810	1,240	1,485	25.8
Morgan Guaranty series for gross size of international banking market[c]	20 E	208 E	1,559	2,253	2,598	26.1

NOTE: BIS is Bank for International Settlements. E—partly estimated by Ralph C. Bryant, Senior Fellow, Brookings Institution.

a. Both the output and the trade series incorporate rough estimates for some countries. "Trade" is a country aggregation of statistics for exports of goods and services.

b. In concept this series nets out interbank redepositing among the banks in the reporting area. The reporting area in recent years has included banks in the Group of Ten countries plus Luxembourg, Austria, Denmark, Ireland, and the offshore branches of U.S. banks in the Bahamas, the Cayman Islands, Panama, Hong Kong, and Singapore. Banks in Finland, Norway, and Spain were added to the reporting area as of December 1983. Only the Group of Ten countries were included in the reporting area in the 1960s and early 1970s.

c. This measure differs from the BIS series for net international bank credit in two major ways: it includes redepositing among the reporting banks, and it defines the reporting area to cover a larger number of countries and banks.

SOURCES: Ralph C. Bryant, *International Financial Intermediation* (Washington, D.C.: Brookings Institution, 1987), table 3–1. Based on data from the International Monetary Fund, *International Financial Statistics,* Supplement on Output Statistics No. 8 (Washington, D.C.: IMF, 1984); International Monetary Fund, *International Financial Statistics Yearbook 1986;* Bank for International Settlements, annual reports and quarterly statistical releases on international banking developments; and Morgan Guaranty Trust Company of New York, *World Financial Markets,* various issues.

FIGURE 1

U.S. Bill Rate, Exchange Rate, and Rate of Change of Prices, 1955–1987

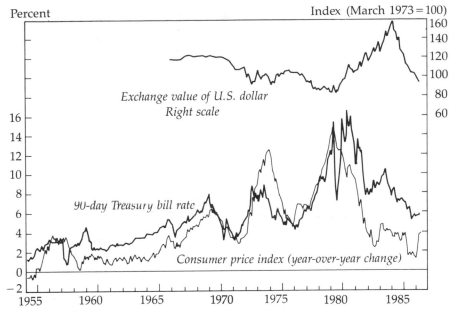

NOTE: *Exchange value of U.S. dollar.* Index of weighted-average exchange value of U.S. dollar against the currencies of ten industrial countries. The weight for each of the ten countries is the 1972–1976 average world trade of that country divided by the average world trade of all ten countries combined. Source: *Federal Reserve Bulletin,* various issues.

Treasury bill rate. Secondary market rate on ninety-day Treasury bills, quoted on a bank-discount basis. Source: Data Resources, Inc.

Consumer price index. Change from same month of preceding year in consumer price index for all urban consumers. Based on data compiled by Bureau of Labor Statistics.

FIGURE 2

Bank Prime Rate versus Interest Rate on Commercial Paper, 1955–1987

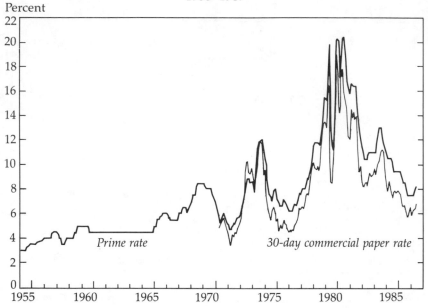

NOTE: *Prime rate.* Prime rate charged by banks on short-term business loans. Source: Data Resources, Inc.

Thirty-day commercial paper rate. Secondary market rate on one-month commercial paper placed through dealers and issued by companies whose bond rating is Standard & Poor's Aa or the equivalent. Rate is offering rate quoted by brokers and dealers, expressed on a bank-discount basis. Source: Federal Reserve Bank of New York.

FIGURE 3
Relative Importance of Commercial Paper in Short-Term Business Credit, 1970–1986

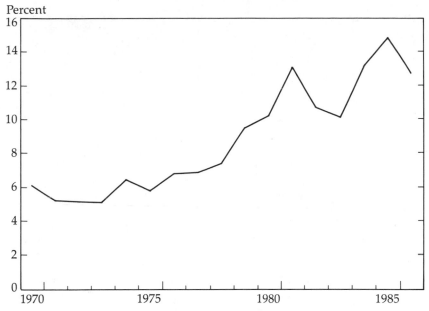

NOTE: Volume of commercial paper issued by nonfinancial companies, as a percentage of sum of commercial paper issued and short-term commercial and industrial bank loans at all commercial banks.

SOURCE: Based on data from *Federal Reserve Bulletin*, various issues.

FIGURE 4

MARKET AND CEILING RATES ON LARGE-DENOMINATION CERTIFICATES OF DEPOSIT, 1964–1987

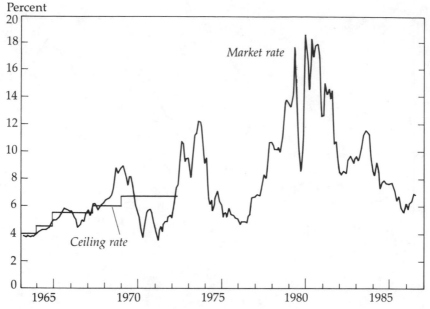

NOTE: *Market rate.* Secondary market rate on large-denomination ninety-day certificates of deposit. Averages of daily figures.

Ceiling rate. Maximum rate on ninety-day single-maturity time deposits in denominations of $100,000 or more. (Before July 20, 1966, maximum applied to smaller ninety-day CDs as well.) Maximums on CDs with maturities of ninety days or more were suspended in May 1973.

SOURCES: Board of Governors of the Federal Reserve System, *Banking and Monetary Statistics, 1941–1970,* table 12.4A; *Statistical Digest, 1973–1977,* table 8; *Federal Reserve Bulletin,* various issues; and statistical release G.13.

TABLE 3
SELECTED MEASURES DEREGULATING DEPOSIT-TAKING ACTIVITIES, 1970–1986

Effective Date	Measure
June 1970	Reg. Q ceilings suspended on large-denomination negotiable certificates of deposit (CDs) with maturities of 30–89 days
September 1970	Federally chartered savings and loan associations (S&Ls) permitted to make preauthorized transfers from savings accounts for household-related expenditures
June 1972	State-chartered mutual savings banks (MSBs) in Massachusetts began offering negotiable-order-of-withdrawal (NOW) accounts
May 1973	Reg. Q ceilings suspended on large-denomination negotiable CDs with maturities of 90 days or more
January 1974	All depository institutions in Massachusetts and New Hampshire authorized by Congress to offer NOW accounts
November 1974	Commercial banks permitted to offer savings accounts to state and local government units
April 1975	Member banks authorized by Federal Reserve to make transfers from a savings account to a demand deposit on customer's telephone order
November 1975	Commercial banks permitted to offer savings accounts to businesses
February 1976	All depository institutions in New England authorized by Congress to offer NOW accounts
May 1976	State-chartered S&Ls and MSBs in New York authorized to offer checking accounts
June 1978	All insured banks and thrifts authorized to offer 6-month money market certificates (MMCs) with minimum denomination of $10,000 and ceiling rates related to that on 6-month Treasury bills
October 1978	Depository institutions in New York authorized by Congress to offer NOW accounts
November 1978	Commercial banks and MSBs authorized to offer automatic transfer service (ATS) from a savings account to a checking account
July 1979	Commercial banks and thrifts authorized to offer small

(Table continues)

TABLE 3 (continued)

Effective Date	Measure
	saver certificates with no minimum denomination but with minimum maturity of 4 years and ceiling rates somewhat below that on 4-year Treasury securities
January 1980	Minimum maturity of small saver certificates reduced to 2½ years, with ceiling rates somewhat below that on 2½-year Treasury securities
December 1980	Commercial banks and thrifts nationwide authorized to offer NOW accounts; maximum rate payable set at 5¼ percent; no minimum denomination
December 1981	Commercial banks and thrifts authorized to offer ceiling-free individual retirement accounts (IRAs) and Keogh accounts with maturities of 1½ years or more and fixed or floating rates; no minimum denomination
May 1982	Commercial banks and thrifts authorized to offer ceiling-free accounts with minimum maturity of 3½ years and no minimum denomination
	Commercial banks and thrifts authorized to offer 91-day time deposits with ceiling rate related to rate on 3-month Treasury bills and minimum denomination of $7,500
September 1982	Commercial banks and thrifts authorized to offer 7- to 31-day accounts with ceiling rate related to rate on 3-month Treasury bills and minimum denomination of $20,000
December 1982	Commercial banks and thrifts authorized to offer money market deposit accounts (MMDAs)—ceiling-free accounts with no minimum maturity but with $2,500 minimum balance and limited transaction features
January 1983	Commercial banks and thrifts authorized to offer Super NOW accounts—ceiling-free transactions accounts with $2,500 minimum balance
	Minimum denomination on 7- to 31-day accounts, 91-day time deposits, and 6-month MMCs reduced to $2,500
	Rate ceiling removed for 7- to 31-day accounts
April 1983	Rate ceilings removed for time deposits at commercial banks and thrifts with maturities of 2½ years or more
October 1983	Rate ceilings removed for time deposits at commercial banks and thrifts with maturities of more than 31 days

TABLE 3 (concluded)

Effective Date	Measure
	and for shorter-term deposits with minimum balance of $2,500
January 1985	Minimum balances for MMDAs, Super NOWs, and 7- to 31-day accounts reduced to $1,000
January 1986	All minimum balance requirements removed
	Rate ceilings and other regulatory limitations on NOW accounts removed
April 1986	Rate ceiling on passbook savings accounts removed
	Authority of federal regulators to set deposit rate ceilings expired

SOURCES: *Annual Report of Council of Economic Advisers,* January 1981, table 11; and Patrick I. Mahoney et al., "Responses to Deregulation: Retail Deposit Pricing from 1983 through 1985," table A-6, Federal Reserve Board, January 1987.

TABLE 4
Volume of Loans Securitized, 1971–1987
(millions of dollars)

	Residential Mortgage Pass-through Securities		Securities Backed by Automobile Receivables	Securities Backed by Credit Card Receivables	Lease Financing Securities
	Federally related[a]	Private issues[b]			
1971	2,767	0	0	0	0
1972	3,156	0	0	0	0
1973	3,276	0	0	0	0
1974	4,597	0	0	0	0
1975	8,397	0	0	0	0
1976	15,126	27	0	0	0
1977	21,940	255	0	0	0
1978	21,570	971	0	0	0
1979	29,486	1,708	0	0	0
1980	23,174	1,115	0	0	0
1981	18,504	1,185	0	0	0
1982	54,152	2,081	0	0	0
1983	83,529	2,754	0	0	0
1984	60,087	2,069	0	0	0
1985	108,368	5,301	898	0	338
1986	258,932	n.a.	10,262	0	175
1987	145,883[c]	n.a.	451[d]	600[d]	119[e]

n.a. = not available.

a. Guaranteed by federal or federally related agencies (Government National Mortgage Association, Federal Home Loan Mortgage Corporation, Federal National Mortgage Association). Excludes securities issued and guaranteed by the Farmers Home Administration (FmHA). Since 1975 all FmHA pass-throughs have been sold to the Federal Financing Bank.

b. Public offerings and private placements of pass-through securities not guaranteed by federal or federally related agencies.

c. Through June: estimate by Board of Governors of the Federal Reserve System.

d. Through April.

e. Through August 7.

Source: Board of Governors of the Federal Reserve System.

TABLE 5

ACTIVITIES APPROVED AND DENIED BY THE
FEDERAL RESERVE BOARD AS "CLOSELY RELATED TO BANKING"
UNDER SECTION 4(c)(8) OF THE BANK HOLDING COMPANY ACT

Permitted by Regulation[a]	Year Added
Making, acquiring, or servicing loans or other extensions of credit, such as would be made by mortgage, finance, credit card, or factoring companies	1971
Operating as an industrial bank, Morris Plan bank, or industrial loan company	1971
Conducting trust or fiduciary activities[b]	1971
Acting as investment or financial adviser[c]	1971
Full-payout leasing of personal and real property[d]	1971
Investing in community welfare projects	1971
Providing data processing services[e]	1971
Acting as insurance agent or broker primarily in connection with credit extensions[f]	1971
Underwriting credit life and credit accident and health insurance related to an extension of credit	1972
Providing courier services	1973
Providing management consulting advice to unaffiliated bank and nonbank depository institutions[g]	1974
Issuance and sale at retail of money orders with a face value of not more than $1,000, savings bonds, and traveler's checks[h]	1979
Performing appraisals of real estate	1980
Performing appraisals of personal property	1986
Arranging commercial real estate equity financing[i]	1983
Conducting securities brokerage activities[j]	1982
Underwriting and dealing in government obligations and money market instruments[k]	1984
Providing foreign exchange advisory and transmittal services[k]	1984
Engaging in futures commission merchant activities[k]	1984
Providing investment advice on financial futures and options on futures	1986
Engaging in consumer financial counseling	1986
Providing tax planning and preparation services	1986
Providing check guaranty services	1986
Operating a collection agency	1986
Operating a credit bureau	1986

(Table continues)

TABLE 5 (continued)

Permitted by Order on an Individual Basis[1]	Year Approved
Operating a "pool-reserve plan" for the pooling of loss reserves of banks with respect to loans to small businesses	1971
Operating a thrift institution in Rhode Island	1972
Buying and selling gold and silver bullion and silver coin	1973
Operating a guaranty savings bank in New Hampshire	1975
Operating an Article XII New York investment company	1977
Engaging in commercial banking activities through foreign branches of a nonbank Delaware company	1982
Acquiring and operating a distressed S&L	1982
Operating a limited-purpose national bank for purposes of avoiding usury ceilings	1983
Operating a nonbank bank through a limited-purpose commercial bank charter	1984
Providing financial feasibility studies for private corporations; performing valuations of companies and of large blocks of stock for a variety of purposes; providing expert witness testimony on behalf of utility firms in rate cases	1986
Engaging in FCM (futures commission merchant) brokerage of futures contracts on a municipal bond index and related futures advisory services	1985
Engaging in FCM brokerage of futures contracts on stock indexes and options on such contracts	1985
Issuing consumer-type payment instruments having a face value of not more than $10,000	1986
Credit card authorization services and lost or stolen credit card reporting services	1985
Engaging in employee benefits consulting activities	1985
Issuing official checks with no limitation on the maximum face value but subject to certain limitations	1985
Providing expanded student loan servicing activities	1985
Underwriting and reinsuring home mortgage redemption insurance	1986
Providing portfolio investment advice in connection with securities brokerage services subject to certain conditions	1986
Printing and selling checks and related documents that require MICR-encoded information for depository institutions	1986
Engaging in commercial paper placement activities to limited extent	1986

TABLE 5 (continued)

Permitted by Order on an Individual Basis[1]	Year Approved
Providing advice regarding the structuring of and arranging for loan syndications, interest rate "swap," interest rate "cap," and similar transactions	1986
Providing cash management services	1986

Activities Denied by the Board	Year Denied
Insurance premium funding ("equity funding") (combined sales of mutual funds and insurance)	1971
Underwriting general life insurance not related to credit extension	1971
Real estate brokerage	1972
Land development	1972
Real estate syndication	1972
General management consulting	1972
Property management	1972
Armored-car service[m]	1973
Sale of level-term credit life insurance	1974
Underwriting mortgage guarantee insurance	1975
Computer output microfilm services	1975
Operating a travel agency	1976
Operating a savings and loan association (except in certain states)	1977
Underwriting property and casualty insurance	1978
Real estate advisory activities	1980
Certain contract key entry services	1980
Offering investment notes with transactional features	1982
Providing credit ratings on bonds, preferred stock, and commercial paper	1984
Acting as a specialist in foreign currency options on a securities exchange	1985
Title insurance activities (3/17/86 board letter concerning Independence Bancorp, Inc.)	1986
Design and assembly of hardware for the processing or transmission of banking and economic data	1986

a. Section 225.25(b) of Regulation Y.

b. Amended in 1974 to narrow in some respects and expand in others.

c. Expanded in 1972 to include advisory services to open-end investment companies.

d. Expanded in 1974 to include real property leases.

(Notes continue)

(Notes to table 5 continued)

e. Expanded in 1982 to permit bank holding companies to engage in data processing and transmission services as specified by the board.

f. Scope narrowed to conform to court decisions in 1979 and 1981; in 1982 it was further narrowed by Title VI of the Garn–St. Germain Depository Institutions Act.

g. Expanded in 1982 to include nonbank depository institutions.

h. This activity was initially approved by order on individual application (1973) and did not include the issuance of traveler's checks. In 1981 the activity was expanded to include issuance of such instruments. In 1984 the activity was expanded to provide for the issuance of money orders as part of the regulatory review and overhaul of Regulation Y, effective February 6, 1984.

i. Activity was initially approved by order on an individual application in July 1982. The amendment to Regulation Y that added this nonbank activity became effective on September 25, 1982.

j. Codifies a previous position taken by the board in acting on an individual application to acquire a retail discount securities broker.

k. This nonbank activity was approved as the result of a complete regulatory review and overhaul of Regulation Y, revised effective February 6, 1984.

l. In approving these activities, the board did so without expanding the list of permissible activities under section 225.25(b) of Regulation Y.

m. Board decided to take no action on this activity at the time courier services were added because the hearing record was inconclusive.

SOURCES: Board of Governors of the Federal Reserve System; Federal Reserve Bank of Atlanta.

TABLE 6
Claims on Foreign Countries Held by U.S. Offices and Foreign Branches of U.S. Chartered Banks, 1975–1986
(billions of dollars, end of year figures)

	Total	Developed Countries	OPEC	Non-OPEC Developing Countries	Offshore Banking Centers	Other[a]
1975	167.0	98.7	6.9	34.2	19.4	7.8
1976	207.7	115.2	12.6	43.1	26.2	10.6
1977	239.4	133.9	17.6	50.0	26.1	11.8
1978[b]	266.2	144.1	22.7	52.6	31.0	16.0
1979	303.9	158.3	22.9	63.0	40.4	19.0
1980	352.0	183.7	22.7	77.4	47.0	21.4
1981	414.3	203.6	24.5	96.2	63.5	26.6
1982	436.1	213.1	26.9	106.5	66.0	23.7
1983	433.9	203.8	28.4	110.8	68.9	22.1
1984[c]	405.7	181.7	24.9	111.8	65.6	21.7
1985	391.9	178.9	21.6	105.1	65.4	21.1
1986	391.9	184.2	19.5	99.3	65.5	23.3

Percentage of Total

	Total	Developed Countries	OPEC	Non-OPEC Developing Countries	Offshore Banking Centers	Other[a]
1975	100.0	59.1	4.1	20.5	11.6	4.7
1976	100.0	55.5	6.1	20.8	12.6	5.1
1977	100.0	55.9	7.4	20.9	10.9	4.9
1978[b]	100.0	54.1	8.5	19.8	11.6	6.0
1979	100.0	52.1	7.5	20.7	13.3	6.3
1980	100.0	52.2	6.4	22.0	13.4	6.1
1981	100.0	49.1	5.9	23.2	15.3	6.4
1982	100.0	48.9	6.2	24.4	15.1	5.4
1983	100.0	47.0	6.5	25.5	15.9	5.1
1984[c]	100.0	44.8	6.1	27.6	16.2	5.3
1985	100.0	45.6	5.5	26.8	16.7	5.4
1986	100.0	47.0	5.0	25.3	16.7	5.9

NOTE: The banking offices covered by these data are the U.S. offices and foreign branches of U.S.-owned banks and of U.S. subsidiaries of foreign-owned banks. Offices not covered include (1) U.S. agencies and branches of foreign-owned banks and (2) foreign subsidiaries of U.S. banks. To minimize duplication, the data are adjusted to exclude the claims on foreign branches held by a U.S. office or another foreign branch of the same banking institution.

a. Eastern Europe, miscellaneous, and unallocated.

b. Beginning with data for June 1978, the claims of the U.S. offices include only banks' own claims payable in dollars. For earlier dates the claims of the

(Notes continue)

(Notes to table 6 continued)
U.S. offices also include customer claims and foreign currency claims (amounting to $10 billion in June 1978).

c. Beginning with June 1984 data, reported claims held by foreign branches have been reduced by an increase in the reporting threshold for "shell" branches from $50 million to $150 million equivalent in total assets, the threshold now applicable to all reporting branches.

SOURCE: Board of Governors of the Federal Reserve System, *Federal Reserve Bulletin*, table 3.21, various issues.

TABLE 7

ASSETS OF FOREIGN BRANCHES OF U.S. BANKS, 1969–1987

(billions of dollars, end of period figures)

	Foreign Branches[a]	Shell Branches[b]	IBFs[c]
1969	33.4	3.0	0.0
1970	42.5	4.7	0.0
1971	52.8	8.5	0.0
1972	66.9	13.1	0.0
1973	98.1	23.8	0.0
1974	120.2	31.7	0.0
1975	131.3	45.2	0.0
1976	152.6	66.8	0.0
1977	179.8	79.1	0.0
1978	215.1	91.7	0.0
1979	255.3	108.9	0.0
1980	277.3	123.8	0.0
1981	313.7	149.1	n.a.
1982	324.3	145.2	64.4
1983	325.0	152.1	82.3
1984	306.9	146.8	85.9
1985	315.9	142.1	90.4
1986	314.0	142.6	80.3
1987	338.4[d]	146.4[d]	81.4[e]

n.a. = not available.

a. Assets of branches in all foreign countries less assets of branches in the Bahamas and Cayman Islands.

b. Assets of branches in the Bahamas and Cayman Islands.

c. International banking facilities (IBFs) were authorized on December 3, 1981. Figures shown are assets of IBFs of large U.S.-chartered banks that file a weekly report of condition (FR 2416). Total IBF assets—including nonweekly reporting banks, agencies and branches of foreign banks, and U.S. offices of Edge and Agreement corporations—were $56.6 billion in 1981, $152.7 billion in 1982, $191.6 billion in 1983, $227.6 billion in 1984, $260.5 billion in 1985, $298.2 billion in 1986, and $295.8 billion in March 1987.

d. April 30, 1987.

e. March 25, 1987.

SOURCES: Board of Governors of the Federal Reserve System, *Federal Reserve Bulletin*, table 3.14, various issues; and Federal Reserve Release G.14, *Monthly Report of Assets and Liabilities of International Banking Facilities*.

TABLE 8

Assets of Foreign Banks in the United States in Relation to Assets of Domestically Owned Banks, 1973–1986
(end of year figures)

	U.S. Offices of Foreign Banks[a] (billions of dollars)	Domestically Owned Banks plus U.S. Offices of Foreign Banks[b] (billions of dollars)	Relative Importance of Foreign Bank Assets (percent)
1973	32.3	855.8	3.8
1974	46.1	944.5	4.9
1975	52.4	988.0	5.3
1976	61.3	1,054.5	5.8
1977	76.8	1,193.5	6.4
1978	109.1	1,356.0	8.0
1979	149.6	1,513.0	9.9
1980	200.6	1,680.2	11.9
1981	250.6	1,862.3	13.5
1982	299.8	2,077.6	14.4
1983	328.8	2,251.1	14.6
1984	394.4	2,482.3	15.9
1985	440.8	2,730.5	16.1
1986	524.3	3,024.1	17.3

a. Data include assets of agencies, branches, subsidiary commercial banks, New York investment companies, and international banking facilities. Edge and Agreement corporations and U.S. offices of Puerto Rican banks are not included.

b. Data include assets of U.S. offices of foreign banks (as in first column) plus assets of domestically owned commercial banks. Latter exclude commercial banks with more than 25 percent foreign bank ownership, Edge and Agreement corporations, and U.S. offices of Puerto Rican banks but include commercial banks owned by nonbank foreigners.

Source: Board of Governors of the Federal Reserve System.

TABLE 9

VOLUME OF FUNDS TRANSFERRED THROUGH
ELECTRONIC PAYMENTS NETWORKS, 1970–1987
(average daily dollar volume in billions of dollars)

Year	Fedwire[a]	CHIPS[b]
1970	30.0	3.0
1971	36.4	4.5
1972	44.0[c]	19.0
1973	57.6	36.7
1974	74.8	42.8
1975	77.2	43.9
1976	87.6	52.6
1977	106.0	64.8
1978	124.0	81.4
1979	193.2	107.4
1980	193.2	147.5
1981	230.8	160.4
1982	296.0	211.0
1983	351.2	240.3
1984	392.0	276.5
1985	436.4	313.6
1986	500.0	425.0
1987[d]	530.0[e]	520.0

a. Electronic payments system operated by Federal Reserve. Converted here to daily averages by dividing by approximate number of working days per year (250).
b. The Clearing House Interbank Payments System, operated by the New York Clearing House Association. Established on April 6, 1970.
c. In 1972 electronic transfer of funds replaced telegrams.
d. Through May.
e. Estimate by Federal Reserve Bank of New York.
SOURCES: Fedwire: Board of Governors of the Federal Reserve System; CHIPS: Federal Reserve Bank of New York.

TABLE 10

Deposit Balances at Commercial Banks and Thrift Institutions and Money Market Mutual Funds, 1959–1986

(December averages of daily figures in billions of dollars, seasonally adjusted)

	Demand Deposits	Saving Deposits	Small-Denomination Time Deposits	Large-Denomination Time Deposits	Other Checkable Deposits (OCDs)	Money Market Deposit Accounts (MMDAs)	Term Repurchase Agreements (RPs)	Term Eurodollars	Overnight RPs and Eurodollars	Money Market Mutual Fund Balances (MMMFs)
1959	111.6	146.4	11.4	1.2	0.0	0.0	0.0	0.7	0.0	0.0
1960	112.5	159.1	12.5	2.0	0.0	0.0	0.0	0.8	0.0	0.0
1961	116.5	175.5	14.8	3.9	0.0	0.0	0.0	1.4	0.0	0.0
1962	118.2	194.8	20.1	7.0	0.0	0.0	0.0	1.6	0.0	0.0
1963	121.7	214.4	25.5	10.8	0.1	0.0	0.0	1.9	0.0	0.0
1964	127.0	235.2	29.2	15.2	0.1	0.0	0.0	2.4	0.0	0.0
1965	132.5	256.9	34.5	21.2	0.1	0.0	0.0	1.7	0.0	0.0
1966	134.6	253.1	55.0	23.1	0.1	0.0	0.0	2.1	0.0	0.0
1967	143.9	263.7	77.8	30.9	0.1	0.0	0.0	2.1	0.0	0.0
1968	155.1	268.9	100.5	37.4	0.1	0.0	0.0	2.9	0.0	0.0
1969	158.8	263.7	120.4	20.4	0.1	0.0	2.6	2.7	2.2	0.0

1970	166.3	261.0	151.1	45.2	0.1	0.0	1.6	2.2	1.3	0.0
1971	176.9	292.2	189.7	57.7	0.2	0.0	2.7	2.7	2.3	0.0
1972	193.7	321.4	231.6	73.3	0.2	0.0	3.5	3.6	2.8	0.0
1973	202.4	326.7	265.8	111.1	0.3	0.0	6.8	5.4	5.3	0.1
1974	207.4	338.5	287.9	144.8	0.4	0.0	7.9	8.0	5.6	1.9
1975	214.1	388.8	337.9	129.7	0.9	0.0	8.2	9.7	5.8	3.1
1976	224.3	453.1	390.8	118.1	2.7	0.0	14.0	14.8	10.6	3.0
1977	239.4	492.2	445.7	145.0	4.2	0.0	19.1	20.2	14.7	3.3
1978	253.5	482.0	521.5	195.1	8.5	0.0	26.6	31.8	20.3	9.5
1979	261.1	423.9	635.3	222.1	17.4	0.0	29.5	44.7	21.2	42.9
1980	265.3	401.4	730.2	259.0	28.0	0.0	34.0	50.3	28.3	76.8
1981	234.6	344.8	825.1	301.8	78.0	0.0	36.0	67.5	35.9	188.6
1982	237.9	357.9	852.8	327.8	103.4	43.2	34.5	81.7	38.8	236.3
1983	242.7	306.6	785.2	329.9	131.3	379.2	51.8	91.5	53.8	181.4
1984	248.4	289.7	887.5	413.9	146.3	417.0	62.2	83.1	56.3	230.2
1985	271.5	303.6	880.3	436.5	178.6	512.0	66.0	76.7	70.3	241.1
1986	307.8	371.5	852.4	444.3	232.7	570.7	81.1	83.0	75.7	291.3

SOURCE: *Annual Report of Council of Economic Advisers*, January 1987, table B-65.

79

FIGURE 5

Federal Receipts, Expenditures, and Surplus or Deficit, 1955–1986

(percentage of GNP)

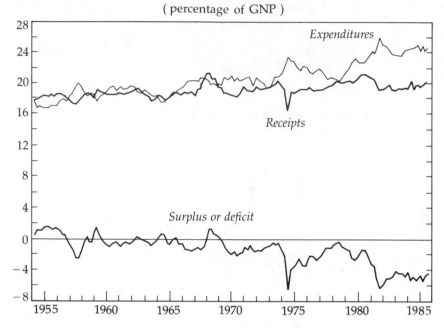

Source: Based on data compiled by Office of Management and Budget and Department of Commerce, Bureau of Economic Analysis.

TABLE 11

U.S. CURRENT ACCOUNT BALANCE, 1955–1986
(billions of dollars)

	Current Account Balance	Merchandise Exports	Merchandise Imports	Services, Net[a]	Other, Net[b]
1955	0.4	14.4	−11.5	2.7	−5.2
1960	2.8	19.7	−14.8	3.1	−5.1
1965	5.4	26.5	−21.5	5.5	−5.1
1970	2.3	42.5	−39.9	6.5	−6.8
1971	−1.4	43.3	−45.6	7.6	−6.7
1972	−5.8	49.4	−55.8	8.1	−7.5
1973	7.1	71.4	−70.5	12.4	−6.2
1974	2.0	98.3	−103.8	16.6	−9.1
1975	18.1	107.1	−98.2	14.8	−5.6
1976	4.2	114.7	−124.2	18.4	−4.8
1977	−14.5	120.8	−151.9	20.1	−3.5
1978	−15.4	142.1	−176.0	23.5	−4.9
1979	−1.0	184.5	−212.0	34.5	−7.9
1980	1.9	224.3	−249.7	37.2	−9.8
1981	6.3	237.1	−265.1	42.9	−8.6
1982	−8.7	211.2	−247.6	37.0	−9.2
1983	−46.2	201.8	−268.9	30.6	−9.7
1984	−107.0	219.9	−332.4	19.6	−14.1
1985	−116.4	215.9	−338.1	24.4	−18.6
1986	−141.4	224.4	−368.7	22.3	−19.3

a. Investment income, travel and transportation receipts, and other services.
b. Military transactions plus remittances, pensions, and other unilateral transfers.
SOURCE: Department of Commerce, *Survey of Current Business*, various issues.

TABLE 12

Debt Outstanding, United States, 1955–1987
(percentage of GNP)

	Total	U.S. Government	State and Local Government	Households		Nonfinancial Business	
				Mortgages	Consumer credit	Long-Term	Short-Term
1955	135.8	56.6	11.4	20.5	11.2	23.6	10.3
1960	141.1	45.8	14.0	26.6	12.6	26.6	12.4
1965	143.5	37.2	14.6	30.4	14.6	28.6	14.4
1970	141.0	29.6	14.7	28.6	14.1	32.2	17.3
1973	140.6	25.7	14.2	29.2	15.0	33.5	18.4
1974	141.4	24.5	14.1	29.3	14.5	34.1	20.2
1975	142.0	27.9	13.8	29.4	13.7	34.4	18.2
1976	140.8	28.9	13.1	29.7	13.7	33.6	17.4
1977	142.1	28.8	12.3	31.1	14.2	33.6	17.8
1978	142.0	27.8	11.6	32.3	14.6	32.8	18.5
1979	142.8	26.5	11.1	33.8	14.8	32.4	19.9
1980	143.7	27.2	10.8	34.5	13.8	32.3	20.2
1981	140.9	27.2	9.9	33.5	13.1	31.0	21.1
1982	147.8	31.3	10.2	33.6	13.2	31.9	21.9
1983	153.6	34.6	10.5	34.5	13.9	32.5	21.8
1984	159.0	36.6	10.2	34.6	15.1	33.5	23.4
1985	171.4	40.0	12.3	36.3	16.7	36.0	23.7
1986	182.6	43.1	13.1	39.1	17.2	39.1	24.6
1987[a]	179.3	42.1	13.0	38.9	16.7	38.8	23.8

a. First quarter, seasonally adjusted.
Source: Based on data from Board of Governors of the Federal Reserve System, Flow of Funds Accounts.

TABLE 13

BANKS CLOSED BECAUSE OF FINANCIAL DIFFICULTIES
AND THEIR DEPOSITS, 1955–1986

Period[a]	Number of Banks	Total Deposits (millions of dollars)
1955–59	5	9.8
1960–64	5	14.0
1965–69	7	45.0
1970	8	55.2
1971	6	132.1
1972	3	99.8
1973	6	971.3
1974	4	1,575.8
1975	14	340.6
1976	17	865.7
1977	6	205.2
1978	7	854.2
1979	10	110.7
1980	10	216.3
1981	10	3,826.0
1982	42	9,908.4
1983	48	5,441.6
1984	79	2,883.2
1985	118	8,059.4
1986	138	6,009.8

a. Figures for first three periods are five-year averages.
SOURCE: Federal Deposit Insurance Corporation.

TABLE 14

EXTERNAL ASSETS AND LIABILITIES OF THE U.S. ECONOMY, SELECTED YEARS, 1952–1986

(billions of dollars outstanding at year end unless otherwise indicated)

	1952	1962	1972	1975	1978	1981	1983	1985	1986
U.S. assets abroad	59.1	96.7	198.7	295.1	447.9	719.8	873.9	949.4	1,067.9
U.S. official reserve assets[a]	24.7	17.2	13.2	16.2	18.7	30.1	33.7	43.2	48.5
Other assets of U.S. government	11.7	19.2	36.1	41.8	54.2	68.7	79.5	87.7	89.5
Assets of private U.S. residents	22.7	60.3	149.4	237.1	375.0	621.1	760.7	818.5	929.9
Direct investments	14.7	37.3	89.9	124.1	162.7	228.3	207.2	229.7	259.9
Foreign securities	4.7	11.9	27.4	34.9	53.4	63.4	83.8	112.8	131.1
Claims reported by nonbanks on unaffiliated foreigners	1.8	3.9	11.4	18.3	28.1	35.9	35.1	28.6	32.6
Claims reported by banks[b]	1.5	7.3	20.7	59.8	130.8	293.5	434.5	447.4	506.4
Foreign assets in the United States	20.8	46.3	161.7	220.9	371.7	578.7	784.3	1,061.3	1,331.5
Foreign official assets[c]	5.0 E	14.0 E	63.0	86.9	173.1	180.4	194.5	202.5	240.8
Other foreign assets in the United States	16.0 E	32.0 E	98.7	134.0	198.7	398.3	589.8	858.8	1,090.7
Direct investments	3.9	7.6	14.9	27.7	42.5	108.7	137.1	184.6	209.3
Securities other than U.S. Treasury securities	n.a.	n.a.	50.7	45.7	53.6	75.1	113.7	206.6	309.5
Liabilities reported by U.S. nonbanks to unaffiliated foreigners	n.a.	n.a.	10.7	13.9	16.0	30.6	26.9	29.4	26.7
Liabilities reported by U.S. banks to nonofficial foreigners[d]	4.6 E	9.2 E	22.4	46.7	86.6	183.9	312.2	438.1	545.1
Net external asset position	38.3	50.4	37.0	74.2	76.1	141.1	89.6	-111.9	-263.6
U.S. gross domestic product[e]	349.5	570.2	1,201.6	1,580.9	2,219.1	3,000.5	3,355.9	3,957.0	4,168.9

Ratio of external assets other than held by the U.S. government to GDP (%)	6.5	10.6	12.4	15.0	16.9	20.7	22.7	20.7	22.3
Ratio of external liabilities to GDP (%)	6.0	8.1	13.5	14.0	16.8	19.3	23.4	26.8	31.9

E—estimated by Ralph C. Bryant, Senior Fellow, Brookings Institution.

n.a. = not available.

a. The U.S. gold stock is valued at $35 per ounce before May 1972, at $38 per ounce between May 1972 and October 1973, and thereafter at $42.22 per ounce. Foreign currency reserves are valued at exchange rates at time of purchase through 1973 and at current exchange rates thereafter.

b. Includes claims on foreign residents of banking offices in the United States owned by foreigners and (since December 1981) of international banking facilities and claims on foreign residents held in custody by U.S. banking offices for customers resident in the United States.

c. Includes U.S. government securities owned by foreign institutions and claims of foreign official institutions on banking offices in the United States.

d. Includes U.S. Treasury securities held by nonofficial foreigners. Also includes liabilities to foreign residents of banking offices in the United States owned by foreigners and (since December 1981) of international banking facilities and liabilities of U.S. nonbanks to nonofficial foreigners held in custody and reported by U.S. banking offices.

e. Billions of dollars in current prices, annual flow.

SOURCES: Through 1985: Ralph C. Bryant, *International Financial Intermediation* (Washington D.C.: Brookings Institution, 1987), table 3–6, based mainly on data from the U.S. Department of Commerce, *Survey of Current Business*, various issues. Data for 1981–1985 have been revised. For 1986: U.S. Department of Commerce, *Survey of Current Business* (June 1987), table 2.

TABLE 15

INDICATORS OF INTERNATIONAL BANKING, UNITED STATES, SELECTED YEARS, 1952–1986
(billions of dollars at end of year unless otherwise indicated)

	1952	1962	1972	1975	1978	1981	1983	1985	1986	Compound Annual Rate of Growth, 1952–86
A. Claims of U.S. banking offices on foreign residents[a]										
1. Total reported[b]	1.5	7.3	20.7	59.8	130.9	293.5	434.5	447.8	504.5	18.7
2. Banks' own claims	1.0 E	6.2 E	15.5 E	51.5 E	119.3	256.6	398.5	418.2	468.7	19.8
B. Liabilities of U.S. banking offices to foreign residents[a]										
1. Total reported[c]	9.3	22.0	61.7	96.2	169.2	247.4	374.8	451.1	567.3	12.9
2. Banks' own liabilities denominated in dollars	6.1 E	11.7 E	25.0 E	51.0 E	78.7	163.8	279.1	341.1	404.4	13.1
C. Total assets of foreign branches of U.S.-chartered banks[d]	1.3 E	4.3 E	78.2	176.5	306.8	462.8	477.1	458.0	456.6	18.8
D. Consolidated claims on unaffiliated foreigners at domestic offices and										

foreign branches of U.S.-chartered banks[e]	1.7 E	7.5 E	71.5 E	167.0	266.2	415.2	433.9	391.9	391.7	17.4
E. Total assets at domestic offices[f]										
1. U.S.-chartered commercial banks	189.6 E	298.1 E	740.8	957.2	1,278.2	1,692.3	2,032.3	2,383 E	2,683[h]	8.1
2. All U.S. commercial banking institutions	191.0 E	302.7 E	763.6	1,004.8	1,380.1	1,881.8	2,281.1	2,680 E	3,064[h]	8.5
F. Gross domestic product (annual rate during calendar year)[g]	349.5	570.2	1,201.6	1,580.9	2,219.1	3,000.5	3,355.9	3,957.0	4,168.9	7.6
G. International trade in goods and services (annual rate during calendar year)[g]	17.6	29.6	79.8	145.8	225.4	365.9	355.6	409.2	433.4	9.9

E—Partially estimated by Ralph C. Bryant, Senior Fellow, Brookings Institution.

a. Banking institutions reporting these data include U.S.-chartered commercial banks, U.S. agencies and branches of foreign banks, domestic offices of Edge and Agreement corporations, New York investment company subsidiaries of foreign banks, and (after December 1981) international banking facilities. The United States includes Puerto Rico, the Virgin Islands, and other overseas U.S. territories and possessions.

b. Includes claims held in custody for domestic customers.

c. Includes custody liabilities such as U.S. government securities owned by foreigners.

d. Series contains minor discontinuities due to changes in reporting requirements. Estimates for 1952 and 1962 are based on end-year condition reports published in Federal Reserve Board annual reports.

e. These data are adjusted to exclude "intrafamily" assets and liabilities (the claims on their foreign branches held by U.S. offices

(Notes continue)

(Notes to table 15 continued)

of a banking organization and the claims of one foreign branch of a banking organization on other foreign branches of the same organization). Reporting institutions include only U.S.-chartered banks.

f. Data for 1952–1983 are based on end-year condition reports. The figures for 1985 were estimated by Ralph C. Bryant on the basis of the last-Wednesday-of-month series. The figures for 1986 were estimated here on the same basis.

g. International trade (in both goods and services) is defined as the arithmetic average of exports and imports. Annual rate during calendar year.

h. Estimate compatible with that for 1985.

Sources: For data through 1985: Ralph C. Bryant, *International Financial Intermediation* (Washington, D.C.: Brookings Institution, 1987), table 3–7, based on data from the following sources: U.S. Department of Commerce, *Survey of Current Business*; and Board of Governors of the Federal Reserve System, *Banking and Monetary Statistics; 1941–1970, Annual Statistical Digests*, and *Federal Reserve Bulletin*, various issues. Certain data for 1983 and 1985 have been revised. For 1986: U.S. Department of Commerce, *Survey of Current Business* (June 1987); and Board of Governors of the Federal Reserve System, *Federal Reserve Bulletin*, various issues.

TABLE 16

INTERNATIONAL BANKING IN RELATION TO BANKS' TOTAL ASSETS AND TO INTERNATIONAL TRADE, UNITED STATES, SELECTED YEARS, 1952–1986

(percent)

Indicator	1952	1962	1972	1975	1978	1981	1983	1985	1986
International banking as a proportion of total assets at banks' domestic offices									
1. Own claims of U.S. banking offices on foreign residents (to total assets at domestic offices of all commercial banking institutions)	0.5 E	2.0 E	2.0 E	5.1 E	8.6	13.6	17.5	15.6	15.3
2. Own dollar liabilities of U.S. banking offices to foreign residents (to total assets at domestic offices at all commercial banking institutions)	3.2 E	3.9 E	3.3 E	5.1 E	5.7	8.7	12.2	12.7	13.2
3. Consolidated claims on unaffiliated foreigners at domestic offices and foreign branches of U.S.-chartered banks (to total assets at domestic offices of U.S.-chartered banks)	0.9 E	2.5 E	9.7 E	17.4	20.8	24.5	21.4	16.4	14.6
International banking in relation to international trade in goods and services									
4. Own claims of U.S. banking offices on foreign residents (all commercial banking institutions)	5.7 E	20.9 E	19.4 E	35.3 E	52.9	70.1	112.1	102.2	108.1
5. Own dollar liabilities of U.S. banking offices to foreign residents (all commercial banking institutions)	34.7 E	39.5 E	31.3 E	35.0 E	34.9	44.8	78.5	83.4	93.3
6. Consolidated claims on unaffiliated foreigners at									

(Table continues)

89

TABLE 16 (concluded)

Indicator	1952	1962	1972	1975	1978	1981	1983	1985	1986
domestic offices and foreign branches of U.S.-chartered banks	9.7 E	25.3 E	89.6 E	114.5	118.1	113.5	122.0	95.8	90.4
7. U.S. international trade in goods and services as percentage of U.S. gross domestic product	5.0	5.2	6.6	9.2	10.2	12.2	10.6	10.3	10.4

E—Underlying series partly estimated by Ralph C. Bryant, Senior Fellow, Brookings Institution.
Source: Derived from table 15. The correspondence between rows in this table and rows in table 15 is as follows (row numbers in table 15 in parentheses): row 1 (A2/E2); row 2 (B2/E2); row 3 (D/E1); row 4 (A2/G); row 5 (B2/G); row 6 (D/G); row 7 (G/F).

TABLE 17
New Lending Facilities Arranged in
International Financial Markets, 1981–1986
(billions of dollars)

	1981	1982	1983	1984	1985	1986
International bond issues	44.0	71.6	72.0	107.9	163.7	220.3
Fixed-rate straight issues	32.1	55.9	46.9	62.0	96.2	145.4
Floating-rate notes	7.8	12.6	15.3	34.0	55.9	47.8
Convertible bonds[a]	4.1	3.2	9.9	11.9	11.6	27.1
Note issuance facilities[b]	1.0	2.3	3.3	18.8	49.5	69.5
Syndicated bank lending[c]	131.5[d]	99.4	51.8	36.6	21.1	37.8
Voluntary loans	131.5	88.2	38.1	30.1	18.8	29.8
"Nonspontaneous" loans[e]	0.0	11.2	13.7	6.5	2.3	8.0
Total of new facilities	176.5	173.3	127.1	163.3	234.3	327.6
Securities-market facilities as percentage of total new facilities	25.5	42.6	59.2	77.6	91.0	88.5

a. Includes bonds with equity warrants.

b. Covers all Euro-note facilities including underwritten facilities (NIFs, RUFs, and multiple-component facilities with a note issuance option) and nonunderwritten or uncommitted facilities and Euro–commercial paper programs.

c. Does not include existing loans newly negotiated where only spreads are changed.

d. Includes $35 billion of U.S. takeover-related standbys.

e. The new-money element of rescue packages arranged for heavily indebted countries by the International Monetary Fund and other governmental entities in cooperation with commercial banks.

Sources: For data through 1985: Ralph C. Bryant, *International Financial Intermediation* (Washington, D.C.: Brookings Institution, 1987), table 3-13, based on data from Bank for International Settlements, *Fifty-sixth Annual Report* (Basel, 1986), pp. 101–7. Certain data have been revised. For 1986: Bank for International Settlements, *Fifty-seventh Annual Report* (Basel, 1987), pp. 107–10.

TABLE 18
Financial Innovations in 1985

Instrument	Description
International markets	
Floating-rate coupon securities	
• Capped	Upper limit on coupon reset rate
• Mini/max	Upper and lower bounds set
• Mismatched	Coupon reset and coupon payment occur at different frequencies
• Partly paid	After initial payment for first part of an issue, purchaser must subscribe to future tranches
Nondollar FRNs	Introduction of deutsche-mark- and yen-denominated FRNs
Nondollar zero-coupon bonds	Introduction of deutsche-mark-, Swiss-franc-, and Japanese-yen-denominated issues
Shoguns	U.S. dollar bonds issued in Japan
Sushis	Eurobonds issued by Japanese entities that do not count against limits on holdings of foreign securities
Yen-denominated Yankees	Yen bonds issued in U.S. market
ECU-denominated securities	Increased utilization in U.S. markets; introduction of issues in Dutch and Japanese markets
Dual-currency yen bonds	Interest paid in yen, principal paid in other currency at a specified exchange rate
"Down-under" bonds	Increased utilization of Euro–Australian dollar and Euro–New Zealand dollar bond issues
Domestic markets	
Variable-duration notes	At coupon payment date, holder elects to receive either coupon or an additional note with identical terms
Zero-coupon convertible	Zero-coupon bond with option to convert to common stock
Collateralized securities	
• Multifamily pass-through	Pass-throughs collateralized by multifamily mortgages
• Lease backed	Collateralized by leases on plant and equipment

TABLE 18 (continued)

Instrument	Description
• Automobile backed	Collateralized by automobile loans
• Revenue indexed	Mortgage-backed security in which interest payments are augmented by a percentage of issuer's gross earnings
Commercial real estate	
• Finite-life real estate investment trust	Portfolio of real estate equities with a specific date by which the portfolio must be liquidated
• Commercial mortgage pass-throughs	Pass-throughs collateralized by commercial mortgages
• Cross-collateralized pooled financing	Pooled securities allowing recourse to other mortgages in the pool
• Rated, pooled nonrecourse commercial mortgage	Publicly rated nonrecourse real estate–backed bonds
Tax-exempt securities	
• Daily adjustable tax-exempt securities	Puttable long-maturity bonds with coupon rate adjusted daily
• Zero coupon	Zero-coupon tax-exempts
• Capital appreciation bonds	Zero-coupon bonds sold at par or better
• Stepped tax-exempt appreciation on income-realization securities	Zero-coupon bonds for an initial period, after which they are converted to interest-bearing securities
• Municipal option put securities	Puttable bonds with detachable puts
• Periodically adjustable rate trust securities	Participant certificates based on tax-exempt commercial mortgage loans
Futures and options	
Municipal bond contract	Introduction of futures contract to tax-exempt market
Options on Eurodollar futures	Introduction of exchange-traded options on futures to the short end of yield curve
Options on Treasury note futures	Introduction of exchange-traded options on futures to intermediate section of yield curve
Japanese government yen bond futures	Introduction of Japanese financial futures contracts

(Table continues)

TABLE 18 (concluded)

Instrument	*Description*
ECU warrants	Introduction in Europe of publicly offered and listed options on ECU
European-style options	Introduction in United States of options that can only be exercised at expiration; in addition, currency strike prices are in European rather than American terms
Range forward contract	A forward-exchange contract that specifies a range of exchange rates for which currencies are exchanged on the expiration date
U.S. dollar index	Introduction of a futures contract on the dollar's trade-weighted value
Options on cash five-year Treasury notes	Introduction of options to this sector of the yield curve

NOTE: Instruments that either were introduced or became widely used during 1985.
SOURCE: Henry Kaufman, *Interest Rates, the Markets, and the New Financial World* (New York: Times Books, 1986).